Eph 3:20 —

REFUGE

MOVING FROM PAIN TO PURPOSE

JIM HALBERT

FOREWARD BY **BILL & JODY BUCKNER**
ALL STAR MAJOR LEAGUE BASEBALL PLAYER

BATTLE AXE
PUBLISHING
© COPYRIGHT 2013

REFUGE
Moving from Pain to Purpose
By Jim Halbert

ISBN: 978-1-938848-36-0

Cover & Interior Design By:
Zac Halbert & Matthew Howen
www.behance.net/matthewhowen

BattleAxe Publishing
2849 S. Palmatier Way
Boise, Idaho 83716

BATTLE AXE
PUBLISHING
© COPYRIGHT 2013

THE PHOTO ON THE COVER

The cover of this book is a photo I took of the front door to the Church of the Holy Sepulcher in Jerusalem, Israel. The church is built over the sight of Golgotha, the place of Jesus' crucifixion. Though people debate the actual sight, there is clear evidence that, from as far back as 60 AD, followers of Jesus gathered there to worship Him. The church was built over this sight at the direction of Helena, the mother of Constantine. It was built, destroyed, rebuilt, and added onto over the past hundreds of years, but when I walked through this door I stopped and considered, this is the doorway to our redemption.

I hope the photo will serve as an icon for you, the reader, to remind you of Jesus' invitation to you to enter into His life.

Jim

TABLE OF CONTENTS

FOREWORD

Into everyone's life a little rain must fall. Trite as that may sound, the truth of it is undeniable. For reasons known only to our Lord and Savior, some people experience more rain than others. The point is, we all, at some point in our lives, go through trials, some small and some major. We don't like them, but it's a pretty safe bet that they cause us pause and reflection. For my wife Jody and I, our trials always bring us closer to God as we seek Him for refuge.

My name is Bill Buckner. I played Major League Baseball for 22 years. I was very blessed with God-given talent, and it was apparent at an early age that I was gifted for the sport. I began my career with the Los Angeles Dodgers and ended it with the Boston Red Sox. Without going into too much detail of the specifics of my career, suffice it to say, there were many ups and downs, injuries, wins and losses, and stress. Baseball is a game of failure with the best hitters in the world failing 70% of the time. Needless to say, one must be mentally tough and have something other than the fleeting and ever changing on-field success to survive baseball as well as life. For me that was a personal relationship with Jesus Christ.

It was 1975; I was playing left field for the Dodgers in a game against the San Francisco Giants. In an attempt to steal second base, I suffered a serious ankle injury. Surgery ensued, complications followed, and a severe staph infection left my ankle very damaged. I was told by several doctors that I would not play ball again.

The Dodgers traded me to the Cubs after that season. I was devastated and scared. In that season with the Cubs, we were in first place by 7 ½ games at the All-Star break. Due to the fact that the Cubs had traded their top player for me, I felt enormous pressure to perform at my best. The problem was, I was playing on a very damaged and painful ankle. I had no business even being on the field. It was then that I met a new teammate who introduced me to God and His Word. He explained to me how God is in control of all things and that with His help all things are possible. It was at that very low point in my life that I accepted Christ as my Lord and Savior. I could not have made it through that season without my faith in God. God chose not to completely heal my ankle, but He gave me the strength and tenacity to overcome the pain. I played baseball for fifteen more years.

It would be remiss of me not to mention the 1986 World Series. For those of you who have not heard the story, google it. There is plenty to be read about it. What I will say is that it was a pivotal point in my and Jody's life and continues to be so. We had a choice then, to allow the situation to make us angry and bitter and live lives of resentment or to draw on our faith and move forward. God allowed it. What began as heartbreak has become blessing untold. God truly does work in mysterious ways. Had Jody and I not had our Lord in whom to find direction and refuge, things would not have turned out the way they have. God used us, and continues to use us, as an inspiration to others, as people of refuge all to His Glory.

When we were asked to write this foreword, I immediately accepted after reading *Refuge*. Clearly the book resonated with me due to its' subject matter. To quote a passage, "A crisis of faith either builds strength and character or diminishes all potential for further growth and influence." Jody and I can certainly attest to that. There is not enough room on these pages to tell of the lessons Jody and I have learned in the wake of '86.

Pastor Jim Halbert also speaks frequently of transformation. He recounts the story of David and how he is transformed by God only when he becomes aware of his own weakness, thus inspiring his men to grow through their own pain—the prerequisite for transformation. Pastor Jim goes on to describe a person of refuge, "he represents God to others, he is continually connected to the King, he is purposeful and practical, he sees life as a mission and he is in a constant state of grace and growth." Pastor Jim closes with the admonition that none of this is possible without full dependence on and partnership with God.

For anyone who needs encouragement in this life and help through its struggles in the context of God and His Word, Jody and I recommend *Refuge*. It certainly encouraged us.

In Him,

Bill and Jody Buckner

Bill Buckner played 22 years in the Major Leagues, primarily for the Chicago Cubs and Boston Red Sox. He had a lifetime batting average of .289 with 2,715 hits, 174 home runs, 498 doubles and 1,208 RBI's. He won one batting title with the Cubs in 1980 and was named an All-Star in 1981. He is one of a small number of players who had 200 hit-seasons in both leagues and played in four decades, but Jim remembers him most when he, while munching on Dodger Dogs, watched him play for LA.

INTRODUCTION

"So David got away and escaped to the Cave of Adullam. When his brothers and others associated with his family heard where he was, they came down and joined him."

I Samuel 22:1

CAN MY PAIN HAVE PURPOSE?

Why do guys often call their private spaces "man caves?" Most men I know don't like being confined in dark spaces, and I concur wholeheartedly. I can't stand caves! They're dark and scary, cold and stifling, and unless you can convince me there's something worth seeing in that dank, unpredictable darkness, I'm just not going in.

After nearly two weeks of trekking through the sweltering wilderness, scaling Mount Sinai to a Bedouin encampment to sleep overnight under a starlit canopy, and crossing the Jordan River at Jericho, I was fixated on getting to the wartime fortress of King David.

The caves of Adullam are about a mile south of where David slew Goliath. This series of underground caverns at one time held upwards of 400 men who were in hiding with David. In one of the larger caves, near the entrance and off the ground about waist high, is a small wormhole shaft leading further into the depths of the earth. This passage can't be accessed by walking; no, this route requires slithering, twisting, and because of my bulky frame, even contorting to make it through the narrow passage.

So, now that I had finally arrived in this place that I had read so much about, I was sweating bullets, but I had to take the plunge deep into the interior of that ancient, eerie cave. Standing in the interior of the larger cave, the nearly 120 degree temperature outside had cooled off to a comfortable 100! My hiking shirt, designed to keep me cool and collected, was drenched with perspiration leaving salt deposits down my back; my hat was soggy and wilted just like my waning enthusiasm. The air was still, and the room smelled stale; I hyperventilated at the thought of heaving this sweaty mass into that tiny hole.

Being in small, confined spaces is one of my greatest fears, but I kept telling myself over and over that I didn't come all this way to quit now. So with laser-like focus, I crawled into the hole scooting on my belly and polishing the limestone with my sweat-soaked shirt.

Some friends I had met on our journey, who knew of my fears, understood how I had looked forward to this day and how much I wanted to be here in the place David hid in fear for his life all those centuries ago. They urged me onward deep inside the tunnel as I twisted, turned, and used my elbows to propel me further in. I did not stop to think; I focused ahead and kept moving albeit slowly, very slowly. With one much smaller guy in front and another behind, I gulped the air, wiped the sweat out of my eyes, and inched into the darkness.

My headlamp was lit but kept slipping down my sweaty brow into my eyes as I exhaled laboriously, slipping down into the cave head first. I attempted to advance on hands and knees, but the conduit was squeezing around me into an even smaller duct as I twisted through the smooth limestone pipe prodded by my desire and the constant verbal support of my fellow spelunkers.

My wife's excited voice echoing down the stone tube far up ahead told me the end was near and the quest was all worth it. Finally I could see the opening and dropped, literally, into a large room. This space, known in ancient times as a columbarium, had a series of consecutive holes lined up like post office mail slots carved into the walls. Their purpose was to house doves that were used to, among other things, send and receive messages across enemy lines. As I stood in the darkness scanning the walls with the beam of my lamp, I was overwhelmed with the thought that thousands of years earlier David probably ran his secret operation from this place. I don't know what David used the doves for, but it was quite possible I was standing in the middle of King David's internet provider!

This was a dream come true. I had written about this cave. I had imagined about this place where a motley crew had gathered with David while he hid from the murderous threats of King Saul. I was determined to reach this place, and now I had. I was reaping the reward of facing the darkness and my fear!

I'll tell you more about the story later, but the metaphor of the cave illustrates how we can *move from pain to purpose* in our lives. Hundreds of men were radically transformed there. They didn't want to be in that cave any more or longer than I wanted to be, but the refuge of this place provided them a new reason and way to live. Pain drew them into the cave, but purpose drove them out.

Like most folks, I don't relish dark, confined spaces or the thought of being someplace I can't get out of. However, I have learned through struggle that some things can't be seen unless we're willing to plunge into the darkness. Once inside, the distant light at the end of the tunnel is both reassuring and illuminating. If we allow it to, the darkness will change us, and we can leave different than we came.

This isn't a story about how to live in the darkness. This is about how a cave turned refugees into warriors. I want the darkness to teach me its lessons, but I also want to move on and out as quickly as I can. Would you be willing to do a little spelunking with me? Turn your headlamp on and take a deep breath, I'll be right behind you.

Tarzan, circa 1966

1

A DANGEROUS OPPORTUNITY

I don't like caves, but they're necessary. They are the safe places where we are free to explore what's wrong on the inside, so we can handle life well when we leave the cave. Growing up in a Christian home, I assumed that the church was a place or cave of refuge. That may have led to my desire to be a pastor. Little did I know that caves can also be dark and fraught with danger.

I was "saved" at the age of six. I remember kneeling down in front of our black naugahyde recliner chair in the living room and doing my best to confess my sins, though I didn't fully know what that meant. What I understood in that moment was that Jesus was supposed to be important to me, and He was, so I confessed, asked for God's forgiveness, and immediately became an evangelist.

I promptly headed over to my Catholic buddy across the street and began sharing Jesus with him. This of course meant trying to get him to come to *my* church, the real one. (Oops, I just revealed my learned prejudice). I had no idea that Catholics could love Jesus or even that they knew the same Jesus.

Other than drawing my first nude at the age of seven (which my mom found) and talking a little girl down the street into a game of "self-discovery," I was mostly a good boy. I didn't lie very often or fight too much, although I confess that I hit my friend Bobby so hard once that his mother never let him play with me again—no really, *ever* again. I also stole twelve hot wheels at a birthday party once from the birthday boy himself, but I met the judgment of God for that—thanks Dad.

I went to church, and at home I bowed my head when my Dad said prayer for dinner. I listened in Sunday school, and I enjoyed the flannel graph lessons of Bible heroes (a flannel graph was a big, flannel-covered board with a Bible story scene painted on it accompanied by felt Bible characters that were moved around the board to tell the story). Of course, I always rearranged the Bible heroes on the board after class so that they would be seen in sometimes compromising positions, but it was funny, and I liked making my friends laugh.

When I graduated from flannel-graph Sunday school, I was demoted to "big church." It was nowhere near as fun. My junior and senior high years were about making friends, staying away from bullies, and hanging out with kids who did and smoked things that I knew were wrong. Somewhere along the line, I lost interest in church.

My parents must have seen this change in me, so they changed churches. They wanted me to have the influence of a larger church with more kids my age. The teenagers all gathered in a youth group on Wednesday and Sunday nights. We had to drive about thirty miles to attend that church, so none of the kids in the teen group were people I knew or went to school with. They weren't mean, but they also didn't go out of their way to include me. So, I walked into church with my parents, and during the first prayer, when everyone bowed their heads, I slipped out the back door. For the next hour I cruised the neighborhood, sat in our car and listened to the radio, walked in the park across the street, and did just about anything I could to avoid actually going to church.

My first girlfriend was a Baptist who tried to get me "re-saved." This was familiar; it's what I did with my Catholic buddy (maybe turnabout was fair play). I guess the Baptist Jesus was a different Jesus than ours. I got mad at her warnings of my "hell bound-ness," and her desire to follow up her evangelism efforts with a makeout session was confusing. I didn't think being proselytized was really all that bad; I just didn't believe in her brand of Jesus.

In my frustration and effort to prove my Jesus was the right one, I opened up my Bible for the first time in years. I was after the ammunition I needed to combat my "Jesus is a Baptist-I'm going to be a missionary-You're going to hell but kiss me one more time" girlfriend. Wow, where had this book been hiding? This thing was powerful! The girl and I broke up, but a new relationship began for me with the Bible. Soon, instead of sneaking out of church, I was purposely making an effort to go.

Our pastor was an older guy, but he was really cool. In the midst of my church-skipping days, I discovered his coolness one Sunday after the service had let out. I'd made sure to get back from my neighborhood cruise in time to join the throngs of blessed churchgoers pouring out the back doors. My eyes met with his, and I smiled and said, "Hi Pastor Lee." He winked at me and replied quietly with a sheepish grin, "I see you when you sneak out of the back row, Jim." I was busted! I thought for sure he would tell my parents, but he never did. How cool is that? Mom and Dad, if you're reading this now, I confess. I wasn't always where I said I was. I know, I know, I'll go to my room now.

For a preacher, Pastor Lee was pretty interesting. He was an old guy, but he had this swagger. He could tell a story that would keep you spellbound, yet he always seemed to put the truth down on the bottom shelf where the kids could reach it. One Sunday night he was waxing eloquently and then stopped mid-sentence. I looked up and met his eyes. After some silence, he said to the 1200 people gathered there that night, "I'm disturbed that I'm not seeing more young men and women giving their lives to full time ministry." The whole world stopped for me *that night*.

On that Sunday night, at the age of seventeen, I knew as sure as I was sitting in that pew, that God was calling me to serve Him full time. It was a miracle moment frozen in time. So, in spite of the fact that I was soon to graduate from high school, magna cum barely, I applied to a Christian college to study religion, *and was accepted.* That was the second miracle! I was passionate about doing God's work. After four years of school, during which I married the love of my life, I took a position as a youth pastor in California, book-smart and experience-stupid. Somehow we survived, and so did the students in the youth group. My wife, Dori, was right beside me doing ministry, and life was good!

It wasn't long after the birth of our son that I realized I wasn't getting any younger. I mean, I was already 23 years old! So, we headed for seminary half-way across the United States. Once there, I was overwhelmed by what I didn't know, and underwhelmed by the difficulty of making enough money to pay the bills. We lasted a year and then came back to the church because it was safe, but this time the church was different than our first experience. We discovered difficult staff relationships and church people who were hard to get along with. We found that our best efforts were not always appreciated, and that not every church was a place of safety, joy, and vision. We didn't last long there either, but no worries, we were asked to come back to the very congregation we first served with right out of college. We *knew* this would be a great experience!

In our absence, things had changed there too. Not everyone was getting along as well as they had before, and we found ourselves being forced to choose sides in some rather precarious conflicts. Our emotions were being yanked around for several months. It all came apart one Sunday morning when the head pastor announced he was moving seven miles up the road to start a new church.

The next Sunday nearly half of the congregation went with him. I wasn't asked to come. Instead, I was asked to stay behind and preach to the remnant. I was devastated by broken relationships, shattered ideals, and Christian brothers and sisters taking shots at one another in an effort to prove who was more righteous. I didn't know Christian people could act this way. I limped along for about a year until the church could find a new pastor.

I left there and became the head pastor of a very small church in the San Francisco Bay area. Like the people we left behind, these were good people too, but I was in over my head. This church was familiar with conflict; they had been through some difficult times with pastors and a few of their own members. They had a legitimate mistrust of pastors, and I was starting to really struggle with questions, anger, and doubt. These factors, along with the pressures of having a growing young family, all contributed to a growing sense of doom within me. My experiences with the church were adding up to a pretty sour conclusion.

I began to resent people in the church whom I saw as judgmental. I also became impatient with those that thought praying for forgiveness secured both a position in heaven as well as a free ticket to spew their not-so-righteousness indignation on others around them. As disillusionment grew, I became more and more angry and rigid. I was living in a poor city full of cultural and ethnic barriers, and I was unhappy. These barriers ate away my hope of getting more new people into the congregation. We did gain *some* wonderful people, and we made some terrific friends over that five year period of time, but nothing could make me happy. I couldn't lift this invading fog of heaviness that was choking the life out of my soul. I was grumpy, resentful, angry, and ready to throw it all away. Then one day, I decided to have it out with God. Oh yeah I did, and boy was He scared!

I yelled, kicked, and screamed. "How could you let this happen to me after all I've given up for you?" I'm embarrassed to admit that I actually thought I had truly sacrificed at this point. My youthful and religious idealism was crashing down around me, and I felt abandoned by God in a church and city that didn't feel safe. There was a raging tornado within me, ripping through my life, shredding everything in its path. Pieces of my life, parts of my dreams, and chunks of hope spun chaotically in a deafening roar, and God refused to rescue me! I was alone, lonely, and madder than a hornet. I was also pretty peeved that I had to be a pastor for God when He couldn't even be bothered to answer even one of my prayers.

I resented the idea that I had dedicated my life to full time ministry when the very one I was trying to please with my sacrifice seemed unmoved by my pleas. I reasoned that if God wasn't going to help me, then I had to find someone who would. I had to take the degrading step of crossing the threshold of a counselor's office. Can you believe it? A pastor, the guy who's supposed to have it all figured out, has to seek help from someone who isn't even a minister of God?

My life had been defenselessly sucked up into a vortex of furious rage that my counselor later identified as depression. As I grappled with this discovery, I knew that I needed to quit church. I wasn't prepared to do anything else for a living, but I had to get the heck out of there before I did any more damage. I was in crisis. The Chinese have two symbols that describe the word for crisis: dangerous and opportunity. The danger was that I would continue on living as I had. The opportunity was that I could walk through the darkness and learn to live differently. The question was: would I ever fit into the church again?

2

A HOLY MILITIA

I'm sure you've noticed that those who call themselves Christians don't all act the same. A whole bunch of them are genuinely nice folks that truly love others. I would describe them as people of refuge, because refuge means something you can trust or find safety in. Then there are others who excuse their bad behavior with the notion that they are forgiven anyway, or aren't being honest about who they really are. People of refuge are authentic and make a church a safe place to be.

So how do we avoid being inauthentic? How can we become people of refuge that others really want to be around? What do I need to do to become a real person who is content with God and life and able to help others? If it were a job, what would the job description look like? The job description simply says: God is currently doing in the world today exactly what Jesus did when he walked this earth, and He wants us to do the same. Jesus was in the business of setting people free from oppression and giving them real life, and in fact, He still is. He heals spiritually, emotionally, and physically. The job description of a person of refuge is to become a partner with God in what He's doing in the world!

Jesus began his three year career by reading from the book of Isaiah as he stood before a bunch of folks who didn't know who he was yet. He rolled out the twenty-five foot scroll and went right to the place that we now know as Isaiah chapter 61, verses one and two. He said,

> "The spirit of the sovereign Lord is upon me, because the
> Lord has chosen me. He has commissioned me to encourage
> the poor, to help the brokenhearted, to decree the release of

captives, and the freeing of prisoners, to announce the year when the Lord will show his favor."

Okay, wait. Jesus was literally claiming to be the promised Messiah by quoting this passage. These people knew that this passage was a prophecy about the coming Messiah and His mission. Rather bold don't you think? Jesus was announcing who He was and what He was doing there. He was either claiming to be God, or He was off his rocker! He was also saying, "this is what God cares about!"

If this is what Jesus was all about, then this is what His followers need to be about. We're all different. We have different abilities, talents, and gifts, but our job description is the same: to partner with God. What's important to Him needs to be important to us. How do we fulfill a job description like that? We need Jesus' help! I know myself pretty well; I'm not very good at making a difference in someone's life when I'm relying on my own strength. I need Jesus to give me the power to do this. I simply have to ask Him for help. If I'm serious, He'll be serious. If you and I both take Isaiah 61 seriously, then we'll encourage the poor, help the broken-hearted, release people in bondage, free the prisoners, and announce that God favors us (translation: He's crazy about us!).[1]

If this stuff *really does* happen, and we can be a part of it with God's help, then it seems we will become the kind of people who others are happy to see. When you walk through the door, are people happy to see you? Think about that. The message of Jesus is called "good news." What about my life is good news to other people? If you and I are good news, we'll be people of refuge. To love my neighbor means I look around and notice the needs of those closest to me and do something about it. We don't have to travel the world to find purpose; we simply need to be a refuge to those standing next to us. If God is really enabling us to partner with Him, then even my family and friends will see it. They know us best and will know if

---

1. Cra·zy [kreyzee] senseless; impractical; totally unsound: a crazy scheme: intensely enthusiastic; passionately excited: Informal: very enamored or infatuated (usually followed by about): He was crazy about her.

we're faking it or if we've really changed. When our friends see us as people of refuge, then it's probably not just a good acting job. We're actually being transformed!

Okay, sounds pretty ideal doesn't it? But what about the church? Do we have to be in the church to do this stuff? I left the church. I didn't want to be a pastor, and frankly, after leaving, it took me awhile before I could even attend. Lots of people say, "I'll sign up for this refuge stuff, but I don't want to do church." I get that.

After my depression hit full bore, I had to get out of the church. I blamed my problems on the sometimes-dysfunctional organization I was supposed to love. There really can be dysfunction in the church, but in my case, the problem was more about my dysfunction. It was the stuff that God used to push me to the brink. He wanted me to get to the end of myself, so I could settle down and get to know the real Him.

The word "church" conjures up all sorts of feelings and thoughts doesn't it? Some have had a positive experience with the church, while others have to grab a paper bag and start sucking air at the very mention of the word. If you've been around people of refuge, then your feelings about church are probably pretty good. You think that God is safe, and His kids are alright. In that kind of environment, you probably experienced God's love and the love of church people in a pretty healthy way. If that's your story, you have a lot to be thankful for.

On the other hand, if you're a hyperventilator like me, let me ask you a few questions: In your church experience, was God someone you wanted to know better or someone you needed to appease? Did the Bible lessons make you to wonder if God had any ill feelings about punishing those who messed up? Did you feel that if you were to *really* confess your sin it would be tantamount to yelling, "Santa Claus is dead!" at the *Macy's Thanksgiving Day Parade*? Did you feel like you needed to do more, work harder, and act better in order to be accepted? Now that I've gotten to know Jesus better, I'm certain He wouldn't have liked this kind of a church either! Did you know that in the four gospels of the New Testament, Jesus only used the word "church" twice? Yup, it's true. Does that mean church wasn't important since it's only mentioned twice? Think about this for a moment. Jesus said to his disciples, his followers, "Follow me." "Follow me" meant more than just walking in His footprints. He meant "mimic me." Do what I do, say what I say, think what I think, love whom I love. So was church no big deal to Jesus?

Both uses of the word church (ecclesia in the Greek language) are in Matthew. The first time Jesus used it He said he would build His church on the truth of the statement that Peter, one of his disciples, just made.[2] The second time He used the word was when He was talking about how people of refuge are to treat one another. He was describing how they were supposed to handle relationships when they had conflict with one another.[3] Yes, people of refuge will have conflict. We all see things from different angles. We can also be fairly oblivious at times and say things that hurt people's feelings. Real people of refuge will live honestly and lovingly with one another because that's what Jesus wanted the real church to look like. People of refuge aren't perfect. So church, according to Jesus, is to be where love reigns, not where unrepentant bullies take advantage of people. Conflict can be solved in loving ways, and when it is, healing and maturity is the result. That is Jesus' plan at least. So why did He only mention it twice?

Church, or *ecclesia*, wasn't a religious term. It was a *political* term. Ecclesia was used in the Greek culture for calling people out from under the thumb of an oppressive government. When an ecclesia was called, people were being challenged to stand against their government in civil disobedience. For example, Dr. Martin

2. Matthew 16:16 Peter said "you are the Messiah (or Christ), the Son of the living
God"
3. Matthew 18:17

24

Luther King not only opposed a political system that continued to oppress African-Americans, he called others, of every race, to stand and march with him. In a sense, Dr. King was calling for an ecclesia by standing against a culture of oppression. American history reveals the power of what an ecclesia can do to change the world.

Today when you say church, it conjures religious thoughts. What do you think Jesus wanted the church to actually look like? Let me put it another way: does the church reflect its original calling to stand against oppression and introduce people to true liberty? Jesus was calling for protest of oppression. Although Jesus desired a peaceful kind, he desired a protest nonetheless. Jesus used the Greek word to describe what the community of His followers needed to look like. The best English word to describe the calling of an ecclesia is militia. Jesus wanted a "holy militia"! A militia is a fighting force of non-military-trained citizens. In other words, regular folks with a deep and holy conviction ready to stand up for their true king. Systems, religions, and even governments that don't set the captives free, open the eyes of the blind, or proclaim that God is crazy about all people, need to be opposed! That's wild stuff neighbor!

Now don't go getting any whacked ideas here. Jesus didn't want the church to take up arms; he wanted it to look different than anything else on earth. When a holy militia is on the loose, hearts are healed, and eyes are opened. People are relentlessly accosted by the crazy love of God. I think that's what church is supposed to look like! When I was a kid growing up in the church, being "called out" meant we were supposed to separate from the world. You've heard it, "we don't smoke and we don't chew, and we don't go with girls that do." We didn't go to movies (gasp), or play cards, and we definitely didn't dance! I actually remember a young college couple in my church tradition who, when asked by a school official about a sexual indiscretion, confessed with great relief, "yes we did, but we don't go to movies!" Can you imagine the damaging effect seeing *Bambi* could have had on this young couple?

Growing up, we defined ourselves as Christians by attending church and by what we *didn't* do. Jesus wasn't calling His followers to come out from the world by physically separating themselves from it. He called them to go *into* the culture as salt and light. Light is welcoming to people who feel like they're in the dark, and salt brings out the God-flavor in life.[4] We may be "set apart" or separated for His purposes, but we aren't to set ourselves apart from the world around us.

God loves the whole world! He called for an ecclesia so that we would come out from under oppressive systems that abuse people, even if they are religious! He called us to follow Him because He was starting a movement that would change the world. He was calling for a holy militia, a force that can radically change the lives of people. That's the bride He's coming back for![5]

Jesus was calling us out from under oppressive thinking and actions that demoralize and dehumanize people. We are made for so much more than what we often settle for. He wants a church that is set free and healed from sin so that it's ready to partner with Him. Those partners impact individuals in the world that He loves. Come out from under the old thinking and follow the job description of Jesus. Now that's church!

4. Matthew 5:13 in the Message
5. 2 Corinthians 11:2 and Revelation 19:7; Interestingly the "bride of Christ" is one of the names given to the church. When I say I love Jesus, do I really want to follow that with, "but I hate his wife?" Maybe I've seen some bad examples, but the bride, or the church, is still the way through which God works in the world. Yes He can, and does, work in spite of it sometimes, but He hasn't given up on her.

3

ANY OLD ROCK WILL DO!

Are you still with me? Let me explain how I think a regular person becomes a person of refuge. The next three chapters will unpack the three necessary parts of what I call Refuge Theology. Okay, if the word theology is freaking you out, let me challenge you with the idea that anyone who talks about God (who He is and who He isn't) is a theologian. Theology is a Greek word made up of two words: God (Theos) and talk (Logos). Theology is God-Talk. If you discuss God, you are theologizing.

Refuge Theology is my "God-Talk" and the result of my wrestling with what it means to be a God-Follower. Just so you know where I'm coming from, I accept the Bible as God's written voice, and my theology comes from this source.

King David is one of the Bible's best examples of a person of refuge. All three parts of Refuge Theology are illustrated in his life. There is a lot of archaeological evidence being continually uncovered in Israel which confirms not only his existence, but also his reign as king. Over the years, I have studied, read, and written much about David's life. I have also walked, hiked, spelunked, and sweat in the very places he did. So, here is his story.

Young David's warrior-career started out with a bang! He was the youngest son of Jesse and the punk-little-brother of a few Israelite warriors who were gathered one day on a hillside about fourteen miles southwest of Jerusalem, known as the Shephelah. His brothers were camped out on the hills surrounding the Elah valley.

The fortress the hills provided, enabled King Saul to keep an eye on the passageway from the Mediterranean Sea in the east and the road to Jebus (later called Jerusalem) to the West. From this vantage point, Saul could also see the hillsides full of Philistine warriors who were looking for a fight. We have a showdown coming, so let me sketch this real quick so you can get your holy land bearings.

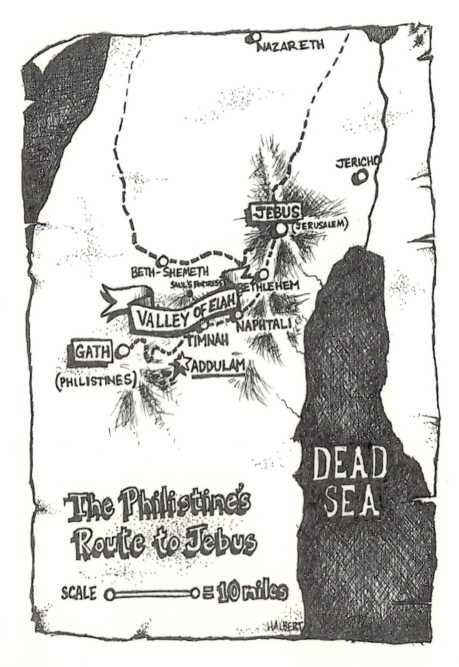

NAZARETH

JERICHO

JEBUS (JERUSALEM)

BETH-SHEMETH
SAUL'S FORTRESS
BETHLEHEM

VALLEY OF ELAH

NAPHTALI

TIMNAH

GATH
(PHILISTINES)

ADDULAM

DEAD SEA

The Philistine's Route to Jebus

SCALE ○———○ = 10 miles

HALBERT

These Philistine warriors came from Gath near the Mediterranean coastal region. The mountain pass from Gath into the valley where the Philistines were is a straight trajectory for the city of Jebus, a key city. Later when David becomes king, he will take over Jebus and change the name to Jerusalem. The focus of our story is the Elah valley, which is about a half to three quarters of a mile wide between two hillsides. At the beginning of David's story, one hillside is filled with Philistine soldiers and the other with Israelite soldiers.

The Israelites were terror-stricken because of one particular and braggadocious Philistine soldier. He was their undefeated blue ribbon bully! They knew the Philistines fought in the Greek style of warfare, man-to-man, champion-to-champion. Their champion wanted Israel's champion to come out and play. Their champion was huge! There he was standing in the valley, looking up at the Israelite soldiers, and calling them out. The Philistine champion came from a family or race of people who were referred to as giants; his name was Goliath. Some early Bible manuscripts gave him a height of almost seven feet while others suggest nine. Either way, the dude was big!

Goliath was teasing the Israelites about their lack of "machismo." He defied their God by saying the Philistine gods could take theirs down. Most wars in ancient times were about whose god was bigger. It was a worldview thing. What we think and say about God (our theology) becomes the glasses we look through to view the world. Come to think of it, most wars these days are about whose god is bigger. Anyway, while the Israelites are getting worn down and exhausted by the taunting, along comes David onto the scene. Young David came to bring lunch to his brothers, but he couldn't help but ask about the beast below, threatening the God of Israel. He was just a kid, but he couldn't believe his brothers and the rest of the soldiers were taking this challenge sitting down.

He was only a young shepherd, but he had asked God, on a

regular basis, to help him overcome the wild beasts that tried to eat his sheep. He had no doubts about whose God was the biggest. He just couldn't believe there was someone who thought he could take on David's God! Courage exploded inside him. It was part rage and part resolve. This giant was no different than the bears or lions he had killed before. Confidently, he asked King Saul why the Israelites were so afraid. David knew the king. He had played his harp for the king whenever depression dampened Saul's spirit, but that's another story.[6]

I wonder if Saul laughed at David's proposal, or marveled at the courage of this kid. David came to Saul indignant but not bragging in his own ability. He was confident that God was going to bring this giant down. David was simply convinced that God would work through any willing servant, and he was the one volunteering! Saul took a chance on David's hair-brained scheme. After being fitted with Saul's heavy battle gear, David wiggled out of it, preferring the old school way of doing things. He would take this giant down just like he had the other beasts that threatened the lives of those he loved. Sometimes the best solution is to do the thing that has worked best in the past. So David, in God's power, took off to face this enemy of God and Israel with his courage and a small leather sling.

Now, let me pause in the story. David never claimed that he could take this giant. He always boasted in God alone. He knew that his best effort would not be enough, but *God's power behind his effort* would make all the difference in the world. You see, David *assumed* that God was real and could be trusted. He believed God would act as he had in the past.

This is the first part of refuge theology. God was David's refuge! He knew God was trustworthy and safe and could be counted on when facing impossible situations. If God isn't our refuge, then our belief in God will be about *appeasing* Him not *loving* Him! If God is mean and unpredictable, then I better make an offering of church attendance or giving money to make sure He doesn't get mad. And if I want to go to heaven, I better make sure that I do more good things than bad things. That's *not* how David rolled. He trusted in God's great affection and fully expected Him to show up on His behalf!

He took off down the hill, through the scrub brush, and over the rocks until he landed at the bottom. At the base of the hill was a dry brook, or a wadi, that during the rainy season ran full and wide. Here is where he usually found the tools of his trade: rocks. They were tumbled and smoothed by the hand of God and perfect for his sling.

Like other shepherds, David used the sling to run off predators and direct his sheep. Small pebbles, flung from a sling, were used to tag the sheep in the backside when they wandered too far off the path. He also used it to run off or kill predators. This time, another "lion" was threatening the nation of Israel. David knew it wouldn't be the rock that dispatched his opponent, but God would be the one to take down Goliath.

From the bottom of the brook, Goliath must have looked even bigger than he had from the mountaintop. He was so close now that David could probably see the saliva spewing from his mouth as he shouted his blasphemous threats. So with one eye on Goliath, David bent down and picked up five smooth stones.

As he rattled the stones loosely in his hand, he felt that same familiar surge of confidence and adrenaline explode inside. It was a burst of holy indignation making his heart beat quickly and his hands tremble. I wonder if he didn't launch right out of that brook and onto the battlefield in a single bound. Why five stones? Who knows, do you suppose David was so confident of God's victory he picked up four additional rocks for Goliath's four brothers?[7]

I can imagine Goliath coming at David, now in rage, wondering what this little punk was going to do. It was an insult for a champion to be sent a kid to battle with. David began to rock his sling back and forth, setting the rock down into the well-worn pouch. He was waiting for that exact moment when the combination of his skill and God's power would fuse. David knew it wasn't the size of rock that mattered because when God was behind it, *any old rock would do!*

We don't know what happened at this point, but Goliath must have been confused by the age and behavior of this kid. As the drama unfolded, I wonder if the Israelite and Philistine onlookers laughed at the absurdity of a shepherd boy taking on Goliath with a sling. As the whir of the heavily weighted sling spun, the moment David anticipated finally arrived. Then in that spirit-led moment, he discharged the stone from the leather thong and waited for the sound of thunder!

First came the whizzing hum of the projectile, then a thud, a crack, and finally a CRASH! A blood-curdling clang on the battlefield shattered the heavy silence. The dramatic scene of victory and defeat was playing out before the Israelite and Philistine soldiers in a surreal slow-motioned clatter of chaos.

Then, before anyone could move, or really knew what had just happened, David was hurtling toward Goliath who was now collapsed face down in the dirt. Goliath was bowing before the real God now. The onlookers were stunned as David pulled the gargantuan sword from the quivering mammoth's hand. With a final thrust of righteous indignation, he quickly severed the giant's head from his convulsing body.

It was mayhem on the battlefield! Hordes of warriors came pouring off the hillside toward David as the frightened Philistines took off toward home with their tails between their legs. In this moment, David taught Israel that their God was trustworthy and a refuge. His contagious confidence in God encouraged others to trust Him too.

Knowing that God can be trusted to do what He says He'll do is essential for a person of refuge. God is safe, consistent, loving, correcting, and committed to welcoming us to live forever with Him. He stands by His word and empowers His children who take big risks to believe God and take Him at His word.[8]

4

WE ALL NEED A PLACE OF REFUGE

Because David had experienced God as a refuge, he became a person of refuge.[9]

We can't fake being a person of refuge because it comes out of an intimate knowledge of God as refuge. If we've really experienced the refuge of God, then the way we interact with others will reflect those convictions. We'll treat people like God has treated us. I like the way David Eckman explains this.

> "The mark of a mature Christian is their ability to sympathize and empathize with people because they have a God who has sympathized with them. That's as much a mark of maturity as anything else. If a Christian is without sympathy that Christian is not mature, no matter how much Bible they know. All they are is a person with a lot of information with hard edges. To know God right is to be a person of sympathy because you've met a God who sympathizes with you. If you do not know the God of the Bible, who is the God of all comfort and encouragement, you may have a God who is just an information database, but He is not the God who humanizes people. He is a calloused God."[10]

Wow that's good stuff! Empathy is not just a sign of maturity, it brings about safety in relationships. The theology of refuge is a spiritual perspective or worldview that asks the question: how can I be to others what God has been to me? A person who lives out this worldview has found that, in spite of their own failure and sin, God's love overshadows their shortcomings. Their sense of being accepted by God now spills over in the way they accept and empathize with others.

9. Psalm 142:5
10. From Tears to Diamonds, Dr. David Eckman. Verbal permission was given to me by Dr. Eckman to print this quote from his talk.

DON'T JUDGE A BOOK BY ITS COVER.

I wish the church was overflowing with people of refuge, but sometimes it doesn't work out that way. One Sunday a teenager came to our morning service with his parents. His hair was in dreadlocks, he had a ring through his lip, and he was dressed in typical skateboarder attire. While waiting for the service to start, people were mingling about and chatting. Apparently offended by this teenager's appearance, an adult churchgoer commented on his attire, letting him know it wasn't very respectful to dress this way for church. The teen and his parents chose not to confront this guy. They told me they were used to comments like that. Man, that hurt!

I was angry. I wanted to set that guy straight! What he didn't know was the kid with the dreadlocks happened to be home from his pro skateboarding tour with the international evangelist Luis Palau. He traveled with a professional skateboarding ministry putting on demonstrations for kids in cities all over the world. After every skateboard demo, these young skaters shared their stories of faith in Jesus and how He had changed their lives. In this young man's short life, he had already seen thousands of teenagers come to Christ, yet he had been judged by his appearance and not accepted! This poor man missed an opportunity to meet a really neat kid, and it's his loss.

It's natural to notice what's on the outside, but we can choose whether to focus on the external or the heart of the person God loves. People of refuge see with God's eyes. Just as God is safe, people of refuge are safe. A church where people of refuge gather needs to be known as a safe place to come where hearts will be seen, stories will be listened to, and outward appearances will be overlooked.

Did you know God commanded the Israelites to provide places of refuge for those who needed someone to hear their story?

He instructed them to establish six cities of refuge throughout the land when they moved into Israel.[11] These cities would provide a place of safety for those who had sinned and needed a judge to hear their case before their avenger could reach them.[12] They were cities designed to be easily accessible within a day's journey from anywhere in the kingdom. Here's a sketch of where they were in relation to modern day Israel and Jordan.

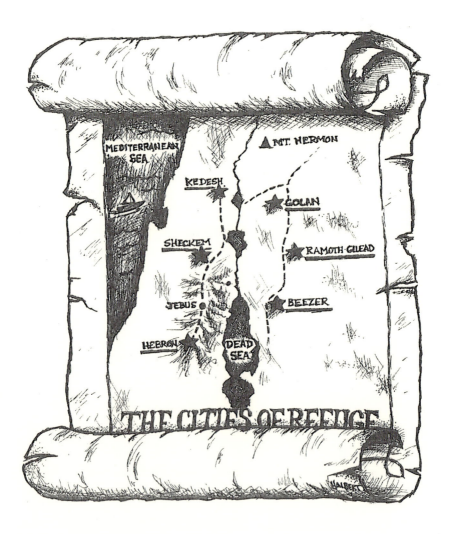

THE CITIES OF REFUGE

11. Numbers 35
12. Deuteronomy 19:1-13 and Joshua 20:1

THE CITIES OF REFUGE

Here's how it worked: a person accused of a crime could rush to the temple in the nearest city of refuge and grab ahold of the horns on the altar. At this point, they were untouchable until they had a chance to tell the priest their side of the story. If after pleading their case the accused was found innocent, they were then provided shelter in the city until that high priest died. At that point they were considered free and could return to their own hometowns.

Okay, now think about what God was really saying here. He was providing mercy, so justice could prevail. Here's what a city of refuge provided:

1. *It was a place to go for mercy.* Mercy is *not* getting what I deserve. Mercy listens before it instructs. Mercy confronts destructive behavior, but it believes in the person. Mercy allows for imperfection while still encouraging repentance and transformation.

2. *It was easy to find and was clear of any obstructions.* A person, as well as a place of refuge, has a supernatural draw for wounded people who are looking for safety. I really believe God sends wounded people to those He knows He can trust.

3. *There was safety at the altar of worship.* This is a reminder of the safety of God. We can come clean with Him. A person of refuge trusts God's work in the other person's life, so they don't arm-twist or manipulate to get people to respond to God. If God drew me to Himself, surely He's capable of drawing others.[13]

4. *The high priest would hear your case.* The high priest took the sins of the people to God to seek His forgiveness. Jesus is

13. John 16:8

our High Priest who takes away our sin because of His own sacrifice for us.[14] Now this is where it can get weird if we're not careful. The Bible tells us that we are to be priests to one another.[15] Though we don't provide what only Jesus can, we are to listen to, pray for, and encourage those who need us. People of refuge stand in the gap between God and hurting people.

5. *You were safe from the enemy.* In a city of refuge a person could live protected from his accuser. That's what God does for us. When God forgives me, it's a done deal. I may not feel forgiven, but I can't live on feelings; I have to live on facts. Satan accuses us of being the people we were, but Jesus reminds us that we are the people He's working in all the way to completion! Accusations of guilt hit us when we're most vulnerable,[16] but God reminds us that He has forgiven us and is committed to finishing what He started in us.

6. *The person could walk free with no fear of payback.* A person of refuge is confident in their forgiveness. With that confidence, they in turn encourage the broken-hearted. They help them to see beyond the difficulties of this life to a day when God and all of his followers will live together. Because that fellowship starts now, Heaven starts now!

David wasn't around when Israel first moved into the promised land and established the six cities of refuge. However, he modeled the very principles of what God wanted those cities to look like. People of refuge are like the ancient cities of refuge in that they provide a place of safety for the broken-hearted.

14. Hebrews 4:14,15
15. I Peter 2:5-9
16. Revelation 12:10

5

WHEN THE END IS REALLY THE BEGINNING

If you've found God to be your refuge, then He's probably met you at some pretty low points. What you learned from those tough times, as you cooperated with what you sensed God's spirit leading you to do, undoubtedly brought about transformation in your life. People of refuge are always in the process of inner transformation.

In the Bible, the word transformation is translated from the Greek word *metamorphoo*. From this, we get the word metamorphosis. As a caterpillar becomes a butterfly, a person of refuge evolves from someone who simply goes through pain to someone who matures through pain. Pain happens in our lives either way, but some of us actually learn something from it.

Here's the deal: people can change. Really. It may be hard to believe that others, or even you, can actually become different from the inside out, but when we trust God, that's exactly what happens. Sometimes before we can change, we need to become frustrated enough to cause a one-eighty in our thinking. Let's let David explain it to us.

David, after killing Goliath, became a fearless warrior, and Israel sang his praises. He advanced in rank in Saul's army, and then he earned the hand of the king's daughter in marriage. As his popularity increased, so did Saul's hatred. As Saul became increasingly jealous of David, he began to plot his murder. Eventually, it became apparent that David had to leave the comforts of home to hide from the king and his fellow soldiers who were commanded to kill him on site. David's thinking was changing. Pain, frustration, and broken dreams were shattering his life and he wondered where God was. He probably even doubted that his past experiences with God were even real. Have you ever been there?

God now seemed so far away and without explanation. David was experiencing the kind of crisis that many of us have gone through. A crisis of faith either builds strength and character or diminishes all potential for further growth and influence. David chose to grow *through* the pain. The confusion and resentment of an undeserved failure can also be an opportunity for maturity. David didn't deserve his circumstances, but he hung in there, choosing to grow and change, which always brings about transformation. David was about to discover that what looked like the end was really just the beginning.

If you're willing to endure suffering in order to grow, you'll learn from those experiences, but no one enjoys the pain of disappointment. Although we can learn a lot in the good times too, it seems that the tough times grab our attention and heighten our sensitivity. It's in these times that we really need to look and listen for God, and David was listening hard!

You see, while Saul was losing his mind, he was also losing his authority. God decided to replace him as king, so he told the prophet Samuel to anoint David as the new king. Saul didn't know it yet, but David knew he was the new king in waiting. And now, here he is on the run, trying to stay away from a crazy king, and confused about his own status. God had chosen him as the next king, so why did he have to hide? Why wasn't God showing up to help him?

This is the point where so many of the Biblical characters discover that faith requires *chutzpah* {huts-pa}. *Chutzpah* is a Yiddish word that means "stick-to-it-ness" or tenacity. It is refusing to give up even when it appears God has forgotten. Chutzpah hangs on for dear life until God shows up. David had chutzpah, and he wouldn't let go until God gave him an answer for his confusion.

David was running for his life and he needed a place to lay low. Not far from the valley of Elah (where he killed Goliath years earlier) was another encampment. This fortress was buried in the depths of the earth. David's hiding place was the cave of Adullam (Au-doo-laum). *Adullam* means refuge, safety, and justice of the people.

This craggy limestone hillside contained a series of caves capable of accommodating a large number of people. When word got out that David was there, a few other broken folks decided to join David to see if they could help him out—four hundred men to be exact! I've crawled through some of these caves, and trust me, you'd have to be a pretty nice guy for me to come live with you there!

David was, in all likelihood, glad to have company. Some of them were family members and some weren't. In fact, a few of the warriors that once fought under Saul went AWOL to join their old comrade David.[17] These four hundred men needed a person of refuge, someone who understood them and could give them something worth living and fighting for. They found refuge in the caves, but more importantly in David. David provided for others what he had experienced from God.

Something happened in that cave. The men that joined David eventually left with David, but they didn't emerge looking anything like the group that had first arrived. They changed in that place. That "cave of safety" where the worn-out found acceptance and healing became a place of transformation. Slowly they unraveled the pain they carried in and were "re-raveled" with a new purpose. What had once looked like the end turned out to be a whole new beginning.

6

FROM MOTLEY TO MIGHTY

In the book of First Samuel, chapter twenty-two, verses one and two, we find the story of the cave of Adullam. The men who gathered with David were in distress, discontented, and in debt. They were a motley crew. If you were going to start an army, these wouldn't be the ones you'd want! The passage goes on to say that David became their leader. Real leadership is not a position as much as it is influence. These men saw something in David that they needed and wanted to emulate. They were broken, hurting, and disillusioned. They were ready for transformation, and David was the influence they needed.

The word for leader used in this verse is *sar*. It means leader,

but it also implies stewardship. To be a steward means we understand that all we possess is God's. A leader-steward understands
that those who follow him or her are entrusted to them and must be
handled with care. David understood that his spiritual responsibility
was to treat these men as God's very own.

The Bible tells us that the men who came to the cave were in
distress, in debt, and discontented. The word distress here is *matsowq*
(maw-tsoke'). It means to be figuratively squeezed into a narrow
place. We might say they were between a rock and a hard place. The
word for debt here is *nasha'*. This is not the debt that comes about
by lack of discipline; rather, it is debt that results from having been
beguiled or deceived. It's being lead astray by those in authority, and
helplessness is implied. The word for discontentment is *mar-nephesh*.
This is a deep, bitter grief experienced in the depths of the soul.
Mar-nephesh can happen when values, morals, and ideals have been
absolutely demolished, leaving a sense of utter hopelessness. These
men were in tough shape.

Deception and bitterness may have defined these men when
they arrived at the cave of Adullam, but they left there a passionate,
confident fighting force to be reckoned with. An utter revolution
happened inside that cave; it was refuge that brought them in, but it
was transformation that enabled them to come out an army.
These guys couldn't keep quiet about the change happening in their
lives. By chapter twenty-four in First Samuel, the number of men
grew to six hundred! If you read on a few chapters, you'll see that out
of this group came David's Mighty Men, the greatest fighting force
Israel has ever known.

What in the world happened in that cave that caused refugees
to become warriors? The Psalms recount David's acute awareness of
his own weakness and God's ability to restore him.[18] Inside the cave
David inspired those men to grow through their own pain. This is

the prerequisite for transformation; God can only transform us when we are aware of and are honest about our weakness. The relentless affection of God is what transforms the human heart. Jesus said, he who has been forgiven much would love much.[19] When we've been loved like this, it transforms us into people of refuge because we see God's daily commitment to our maturity.[20]

My transformation by the love of God is what gives me a passion to help others who haven't experienced this. If I have sin that I am allowing to set up camp in my life, then I need to confess it, own it, and then repent. But, there's a difference between repentance and confession. Confession really isn't hard. It's no big deal to say, "Yup, I did it." To repent means I get off of the path I'm walking and get back onto the path of God. Now that's different, but that is where I really encounter God. When I say, "I don't want this path anymore, I want your's, God," God steps in and empowers our desire.

God is loving, kind, and merciful; His love is crazy when you think about it. We don't deserve it, but we have it. Transformation doesn't happen on my terms. *Transformation happens when I own it, leave it, and get back to having God in charge*—period.

God won't impose Himself on us. The very word "called" means invited, not coerced. If we don't want Him to reign and be in charge, He won't make us submit. It's one of the greatest acts of His love. In the final judgement that the Bible talks about, God will give each of us what we truly desire. If we want to live *without* Him in this life, He won't require us to live *with* Him in the next.[21] He doesn't send anyone to hell; He wants everyone to come to the knowledge of the truth and be saved.[22] If we choose the hell of an eternal separation, He won't stand in our way. Transformation is a choice! If I want to be transformed, I need to live under His care and direction. I cannot serve two masters. Either God is God of my life, or I am god; I simply can't have it both ways.

19. Luke 7:47
20. II Corinthians 3:18
21. Matthew 25:31-46
22. 1 Timothy 2:4

OK, wait a minute. We all struggle with wanting to be autonomous don't we? I would guess that to some degree, yes. Though for some of us, the struggle may be pretty intense. When control becomes essential for me and impossible to give up, there's hope. This intense need to control may indicate an injury from the past that caused great personal harm or danger. The need for control may be coupled with the fear that if we let go, we'll get taken advantage of again. Maybe someone crossed an emotional, physical, or sexual boundary with us and we concluded: "This will never happen to me again!" This kind of pain not only needs to be healed by God, it may also require the help of a professional, or maybe a person of refuge who has walked through the process of transformation. We who struggle with control can have even that healed. Don't let shame keep you from asking for help; God doesn't want you to be misused or abused either. He will help you.

So what about the guys in the cave? How did they change? I don't know, but here's my hunch. David wrote Psalm fifty-seven about his cave of Adullam experience. He reveals six things in this Psalm that seemed to have made the difference in these men's lives.

1. *God alone is the refuge.* We cannot point to ourselves as the source of hope; we must point to God. Only He can restore, forgive, and transform us. David cried out to God, "For in *you* my soul takes refuge."[23]

2. *For God to work in us and through us, transformation is required.* God had a plan for the nation of Israel, to prosper them, not to harm them, and to give them a future.[24] But, Israel's rejection of God kept running them into the ditch of despair, preventing Him from blessing them the way He wanted to. My stubbornness can actually prevent God's blessings in my life? Wow. When I cooperate with God and His transforming work in my life, I am opening myself up to

23. Psalm 57:1 italics mine
24. Jeremiah 29:11

the blessings He intends for me. It was God and good friends that helped these men change. C. S. Lewis once said, "I don't doubt that the Holy Spirit guides your decisions from within when you make them with the intention of pleasing God. The error would be to think that He speaks only within, whereas in reality He speaks also through Scripture, the Church, Christian friends, books etc."[25] God will use whatever and whomever to assist in our transformation. We need one another!

3. *The kingdom of God will permeate a godless culture.* David brags on God to his men. He says, "I am in the midst of lions…let your glory be over all the earth." What he means is God will win even though our enemies look unconquerable. That kind of faith is contagious. David is saying, "Hey guys, God rules!" We are called Ambassadors of Christ. This means we say to the world, "God rules, and He loves you."[26] David understood that the cave of Adullam was a temporary resting place. He knew that for the purposes of God to be fulfilled in his life, he would have to take a stand in the godless culture that was trying to tear him down. These six hundred men caught on to that way of thinking.

4. *Worship helps us discover our purpose.* David woke up in the cave with worship on his mind. Worship perfects and transforms us.[27] Worship is one way God gains access to our hearts. When David worshiped, these men were affected. Think back to his very first encounter with King Saul; it was his harp playing that eased Saul's depression. The song sung in the heart of a person who is radically transformed becomes a catchy tune for those who need to hear God sing over them.[28] People of refuge have heard God sing and can't

25. Wayne Martindale, and Jerry Root, The Quotable Lewis (Wheaton, IL: Tyndale House Publishers, Inc., 1990), 264.
26. II Corinthians 5:20
27. Hebrews 10:1
28. Zephaniah 3:17 NIV

wait to sing God's praise to others.[29]

5. *If God is the refuge, then we can leave the cave!* Caves are great. They hide us from the cruel outside world for a time while we heal. But these men were not called to be cave-dwellers. They were called to be partners with David in establishing a new kingdom. They didn't need to hide because they knew God went with them. Refuge isn't found in a place or an experience; it is found in God alone.

6. *The goal of a person of refuge is to glorify God.* The cave provided a place to gather, to heal, and to understand their calling. Then it was time to walk boldly into the light and proclaim the truth. Jesus said that his followers were to be light that exposes the darkness and salt that brings out the God-flavors in life.[30]

The men who gathered with David that were once distressed, in debt, and discontented found their new identity in God. They were no longer the motley crew who dragged themselves into the cave; they were the mighty men ready to proclaim, "There's a new king in town!"

One of the most amazing stories of transformation I've witnessed happened to a couple of friends of mine. Ron and Cindy were doing their best to make life, marriage, and family work, but they just couldn't do it. What happened to them is all too common, but what eventually happened to them is a rare example of real transformation. They've given me permission to share their story with you. Ron and Cindy came into my office looking like a typical couple in distress. They had two kids, two jobs, and years of marriage under their belt. They sat down and began to unfold the drama. The problems didn't seem insurmountable, but the culprit was Ron's infidelity with the bottle.

Ron had a choice to make: alcohol or his lovely wife and two wonderful children. It was a no brainer for him. He was a drinker, but he wasn't an idiot. He volunteered to quit right there on the spot. Cindy looked at me and then at him and said, "You've told me that before." "This time I mean it, Honey," was his quick response. I encouraged him to get in with an AA meeting, but he said he could handle it on his own, and they left my office.

It wasn't long until they were back again, and, you guessed it, he didn't handle it. This time Cindy was serious. She told him she wanted a divorce. We continued to talk a few more times, and it became evident that Ron had indeed traded his family for the bottle. They soon divorced. Ron hit the bottom of the barrel and finally started attending AA meetings.

In the early days of his recovery, Ron asked me if I thought he could ever win Cindy back. I remember my reply: "Are you getting free from alcohol to bargain with God, or are you doing it because it's the right thing to do?" He nodded. He got it. Ron knew he had crossed the line with Cindy, and he vowed to be the best ex-husband he could be. The results of his life now were completely up to God.

He was there to take the kids when it was his turn. He volunteered to babysit when she went out on dates. Ron was growing by leaps and bounds. He wasn't treating Cindy with kindness and respect to get back what he'd lost; he was doing it because he and God were on a journey of growth together. My respect for him went sky-high. They were both learning to adjust to their new lives, and Ron was practicing being a happy and helpful ex-husband and rejoicing that God still allowed him to have his kids.

Then it happened. He told me one morning over two scrambled egg-beaters with one biscuit and gravy (I know, I know. Trust me, they counteract each other. It's healthy, really it is!). Cindy had invited him to join her and the kids on an event, and he was thrilled.

That one event then turned into several.

Ron and Cindy came to my office to discuss their family situation. They'd both moved on and learned how to live the single life, with the exception of their shared children. With frustration in her voice, Cindy said to me, "If he had been this way before, I never would have divorced him!" I looked at him; he shrugged his shoulders and said, "She's right." They asked a question that I'll never forget: "Do you think it's okay if we date occasionally?" "Yes you're divorced, of course you're free to date," I said. "No," they replied, "We mean date each other."

Ron really did change. He was truly transformed. He wasn't transformed so that he could win Cindy back; he was transformed because he decided to let God take the pain of his life and use it to mature him. His days of conniving and manipulating were over; he was just trying to be what God wanted him to be. Unbeknownst to Ron, Cindy found that attractive...imagine that.

You know how the story ends right? We did it with style though. I asked them if we could use their story to illustrate God's goodness. They both said, "We'll tell our story to anyone if it will cause them to turn to God and trust Him. The glory is ALL His." On a Sunday morning during my preaching time, I invited Cindy up to answer a few questions. They were direct questions like, "Did you divorce Ron?" "Was he an alcoholic?" She replied, "Yes." It was awkward; you could feel the tension in the room. Then I invited Ron to come up. You could literally hear the gasps. I asked him, "Are the things Cindy said true?" He said, "Every bit of it." I then proceeded to ask them both what God had done in their lives. As they shared, the place exploded in applause! I asked them if there was any reason why they shouldn't re-marry. They shrugged their shoulders, looked at each other, and said, "No."

Meanwhile my wife had slipped unnoticed (because every

eye was glued on Ron and Cindy) to the piano bench. As she began to play the wedding march, the congregation broke into another round of tear-filled, spontaneous applause. I choked past the vows and pronounced them husband and wife for the second time! The crowd went wild, the honeymoon-giving box was stuffed with cash, and Ron and Cindy headed out the door to re-begin their life together.

Every time I see them, I remember that God really can and does transform people from the inside out. People change. No seriously, they really can! And they move out into purposeful living as a result of that transformation. They become partners with God.

7

PARTNERING WITH GOD

David was absolutely convinced that God was his refuge and strength. He trusted God when he took out Goliath with that little rock powered by the hand of God, and he gave God the credit as he soared in popularity as Israel's imminent King. In the depths of disappointment following a bitter betrayal, He cried out to God, and God answered him. Experience taught David that God could be trusted and transforms lives.

In the cave David inspired his men to turn to God so that they could be transformed from the inside out. Those men emerged as warriors ready to partner with God. It's the same for us. We move from pain to purpose when, as healed and transformed people, we join God in what he is doing in the world. To move from pain to purpose means I can't just hang out in the cave with other cave-dwellers. In order to partner with God, two things are essential: I must know in the core of my gut that God is truly safe, and I have to be convinced of His merciful love. God has a deep affection for every one of us! We've been called for a purpose! Do you believe that?

When we've experienced mercy, we're going to show it to others. When we've been transformed, we know it wasn't because of our strength, ingenuity, and brilliance; it was because God was faithful. Recognizing God's hand with honesty and humility will keep us from doing something stupid like taking the credit for our transformation. Real authentic transformation is noticed and attractive to hurting people. It draws them like a magnet to God, the only one who can heal our souls. We can say, like Ron and Cindy did, "Lord if you can use my life, my failure, my story, or my gifts to bring someone else closer to you, then let's do this thing!"

Partnership with God isn't a have-to, it's a get-to! We *get to* partner with God by making ourselves fully available to Him. Oh, and by the way, if you're going to partner with God, you better keep your hands inside for the remainder of the ride because it's gonna get wild! When those warriors left the cave of Adullam, they partnered with David to establish a new kingdom. David became the king of Judah, and seven years later he became the king of Israel. As a partner with God, David brought peace to Israel. Under his leadership and care, those mighty men of Israel were given something to live for, to fight for, and even to die for.

First Chronicles chapters eleven and twelve gives us a glimpse into the ways these men partnered with David and God. Remember: they started out in debt, in distress, and discontented. These men were in legitimate pain. That pain was transformed into a purpose and a calling.

There was Jashobeam who became the chief of the mighty men and a leader among his peers. Then the former refugee Eleazar took a courageous stand defending the land from the Philistines when no one else would. There was also the story of the three mighty men who, out of a desire to bless David, risked their lives breaking through the enemy line to retrieve a drink of water from the well of Bethlehem. Their courage so moved David that he poured the water out before the Lord as an offering. Abishai became a commander, and Benaiah was known as a doer of great deeds.

These men and others came to Adullam in support of David and joined their hearts to his. They served him until the day they died. What a picture of partnership. What about you and I? Can we come alongside of our King, helping Him in His agenda to love the world? Can we join our hearts to Him and allow Him to turn our pain into purpose?

As I read the story of David and learned about how he ascended the throne with the help of the mighty men, I realize that truly transformed people can change the course of history. What would happen if everyone who had been through pain allowed God to use that pain for a purpose? I think the world would be impacted tremendously. There are some principles and tangible lessons in this story that we can apply to our own lives.

1. *A person of refuge actually represents God to others.* David became known as a man after God's heart. He represented a merciful loving God in the way he lived and in the words he wrote. This lines up with the scripture telling us that we are ambassadors *for* Christ; we are to actually act and speak on behalf of God.[31] This is a big time responsibility and a high calling. We can actually participate with God in helping people reconcile with Him and one another. If I listen and watch, God will lead me to those opportunities.

2. *A person of refuge is continually connected to the King.* The mighty warriors didn't thank David and then head off into the world to start their own empires; they stayed in constant connection to their king. Jesus is the one who asks us to follow Him. He is the One we're all about. I want to stay in constant contact with Him through his Word and prayer, so He can shape my values, morals, and thinking patterns. Without this melding of our hearts with Jesus, we won't be in partnership with Him.

3. *A person of refuge is purposeful.* There was a kingdom to establish, and the mighty men helped David do this. To offer myself as an instrument in God's hands, I have to be purposeful in becoming all He wants me to be. I want to know His agenda, and I want to surrender mine until eventually they become the same thing.

4. *A person of refuge is practical.* The mighty men were gifted in different ways. We're all different, and our experience and skill set will probably be the best way to partner with God. Maybe we don't need to do anything in addition to what we are already doing, but we will do it differently. Our agenda has changed. Our goals are different. God's plan is to love the world, so I will need to figure out how to partner with Him by using the skills and gifts and relationships I already have. This can be as simple as treating people with respect and as complex as taking on the world systems that oppress the people Jesus died for. Either way, our call to partnership is probably doing what we already do but doing it differently. I still hang out with friends, but now I do it intentionally. I am still a parent, but I engage with my kids and spouse differently. I'll probably still work at the same place, but I'll see my purpose and relationships differently. In essence, I won't become a different person; I'll simply become a practically purposeful person.

5. *A person of refuge sees life as a mission.* David lived to serve God. His whole life was focused on helping to establish Israel as a blessing to the world. He believed the people of God were here on earth to represent the true God. Serving God is not something we do; being a servant is something we *are.* Our status has changed. My life, my relationships, my hobbies, and interests are all given over to the agenda of God's kingdom. I don't have to come up with a vision; I just need to do the next right thing. Jesus is orchestrating this whole thing, and partnership means I'm simply available to Him at all times.

6. *We are in a constant state of grace and growth.* David finished well. He lived for God his entire life, but he did sin. We'll talk

about that soon. This side of heaven, we will not "arrive" or become perfect in our Christ-like character. Like David, we will all know what brokenness feels like. Authentic people of refuge know that grace is what forgives and saves them. But they also know it is the fuel they need for daily living. Partnership is not possible unless we're leaning, with all of our weight, against the one who has promised to come alongside us and lift us up. Grace keeps us going.

I've been trying to stay honest and dependent on God ever since my personal crash. I learned that I was unable to make it on my own, but dagnabit if I don't relapse sometimes and try and do it by myself! The temptation to think my wisdom, ideas, and plans are better than God's requires a daily decision to partner with Him.

Partnering with God is a conscious decision that we must make daily. I need tangible reminders of this truth on a daily basis. When I stray off the path of God, I do so knowing that I'm choosing to give into some thought, urge, or fear instead of calling out to God. God provides a way out of temptation, but He doesn't carry us out! We have to take His hand.

Remembering my ABC's is how I make the conscious daily decision to partner with God. The acronym ABC reminds me of who I am, how I am to live, and what I've been called to. I've even written these letters on my hand at times to constantly remind of the truth—I call it my palm pilot.

The A stands for "Acquired." Acquired is another way of saying purchased or redeemed. I was bought with the price of Jesus' blood.[32] Since he paid a dear price for me, I'm no longer my own. I'm not autonomous. I'm not free to do whatever I want with my body or my life. I live by permission. It's not like Jesus is a mean taskmaster who cracks the whip and keeps me trembling in fear—no. He loves me. Therefore, my body and next breath are His. Before I use my body to do with it what I want, I need to check with my owner first.

The B stands for "Battle-Ready." If I don't own my body, then I need to prepare it for whatever He needs it for. My body needs to be ready for the battle of partnering with God in His kingdom. What if my lack of self-discipline could actually hinder God's ability to use me in a certain situation? Of course, no discipline is fun, but those who are trained by it get to do fun things![33] I want to be trained and ready to join in on what God is doing.

Finally, the C stands for "Comforter-Reliant." The Bible describes the Holy Spirit in many ways, but one of those is "The Comforter." To be "Comforter-Reliant" means I need God not just when I'm down, but when I'm tempted to do wrong. Let me shoot straight. When I sin, I'm fully aware of what I'm doing. Sin rarely sneaks up on me. Sin separates us from the heart of God, and it messes up the process of transformation and partnership. Most of my sins are out of a desire for comfort as well. Instead of choosing my own rendition of comfort, I can choose "The Comforter" who wants to come alongside of me and give me strength. He wants to use me, but if I'm not prepared and battle-ready, I'll miss out.

We get to partner with God, and He loves working through us. There's nothing better than to ask and be put in a place where I can be of some help to a person God loves. Maybe I get to offer a word of encouragement. Maybe my gracious attitude and the generous tip I leave behind is just what that waitperson needed today. Maybe I'm able to use my insights, talents, positions, and influence to make a change that helps other people experience freedom. The possibilities are endless.

After my crisis and leaving ministry, I did several things to feed my family, including using my artistic skills to paint murals in people's homes. It was in doing this simple act that I was able to partner with God and bless someone who had been through severe pain.

"I'M JUST A PAINTER!
HOW CAN I BE A PERSON OF REFUGE?"

While browsing for bargains in a consignment store with my wife one spring afternoon, I looked up and noticed an attractive woman with a puzzled expression on her face looking directly at me. She didn't look familiar, so I thought nothing of it and went back to my bargain hunting. A minute or two later I noticed she was headed my direction. Timidly she spoke my name, smiled warmly, and explained.

"I'm sure you don't recognize me, but I remember you. My name is Janet, and fifteen years ago you painted a mural on my wall. I've never forgotten what you told me that day." The pregnant pause was awkward as I searched my mental data bank trying to remember her and the apparently memorable statement I had made. I sure hoped it was good!

As a painter I created murals, and my canvases were the walls in people's homes. Personally I had been through some painful and difficult situations and I cared deeply about people, especially hurting people. I was a painter, but I also knew God wanted to use me in the lives of others. One day I got a call from Janet asking me to create a Trompe L'oeil mural on her master bedroom wall. Trompe L'oeil means "fool the eye" in French. She wanted a realistic garden scene painted on the wall she would see first thing each morning when she woke up.

She was recently widowed with two teenage kids and trying to put her life back together again. She had been weeping through the first months of getting used to life without her husband and was trying to move on. Redecorating her home was part of the healing process for her. Janet wanted to change things up by creating some new space and memories. She wanted this scene to be a daily reminder of life's beauty and an invitation to enter into it with gratefulness each morning.

I understood what she wanted. More than that, I felt what she really needed. She needed hope, and she wanted to be reminded of the importance of moving forward for the sake of her children and loved ones. I got a picture in my mind and started creating.

At the end of each day's work, I covered the painting so I could surprise her with the final result. An English garden scene began to emerge with a winding path inviting the observer into the woods that lay just beyond the garden. In the foreground I painted an ivy covered rock wall with an iron gate. On the top of each of the gateposts, I added two ornate cherubs to stand guard over those who entered this place of peace. She didn't ask for the angels, and I didn't tell her why I painted them there.

I remember her tears when she saw the finished painting. I explained my interpretation of the garden scene and finally my reason for placing the cherubs on top of the gateposts. "You've been through a very difficult time in your life," I explained. "I painted these to remind you that God places his angels in charge over us. I think it's important that the first thing you see each morning is not just beauty but also the reminder that you matter to God and that He cares."

She wept as she thanked me. Though I had worried that a "religious" symbol like this might be offensive, I took the chance that she would be comforted by it instead. I gathered up my brushes and headed out the door. I never saw her again until the day she called my name from across a consignment store as my wife and I stood there in silence.

Janet reminded me of the painting and the angels. She went on to say what an encouragement that picture had been to her as she walked through her recovery. Tears welled up in her eyes just like they had the day she saw the painting for the first time. She thanked me again for reminding her that God cares.

This story reminds us that *anyone* can be a person of refuge. Partnering with God becomes an opportunity to touch the lives of those He's most concerned about. We get to be God's hands and heart when we're looking for ways to encourage the broken-hearted.

David was successful as a partner with God. He was called a man after God's own heart. Wow, wouldn't that be cool if they said that of you and me? David wasn't perfect, nor are we. But our hearts, like the hearts of David's men, can be united to Jesus' heart. We can join Him as partners in the great task of influencing the world with His love.

8

I CAN'T STOP SWINGIN' THE SWORD!

"The one spiritual disease is thinking that one [is] quite well."[34]

I wish David's story ended with his recovery from the cave, but it doesn't. Good people fail; they even sin. David started relying on his own wisdom, and he took a great fall. When we resist the continual transformation that God is doing in our lives, we set ourselves up for disaster just as David did.

"At that time of year when kings go off to war, David stayed home."[35] This is one of the scariest verses in the Bible. David, the man who had killed Goliath and stopped the Philistines, the one who led his men to become great warriors, decided to stay home from the battle. He was a great man and partner with God. He was self-aware, sensitive to God's gentle whisper, and a prolific writer, penning his innermost thoughts, fears, and joys. He was a man's man and a man after God's own heart, and he was, unfortunately, a woman's man too.[36] So why did he stop swingin' the sword?

Maybe he thought he deserved a break. Maybe he was bored and just tired of being good. Maybe the rigors of daily transformation just got tiring. It's possible that his men's loyalty prevented them from risking the life of their beloved leader in battle.[37] Whatever the reason, David made a dangerous choice when he separated himself from his friends. With no battle plans to make or scoundrels to annihilate, David decided to kick back, let his hair down, and just be himself. All alone in his palace, he was free to enjoy some alone time, unbothered by the pressures of life.

From the rock paved terraces he could gaze to his left over

---

34. G.K Chesterton: The Innocence of Father Brown
35. Samuel 11:1
36. 1 Samuel 13:14, Psalm 89:20, Acts 13:22
37. 2 Samuel 21:17

the Kidron Valley and see the Mount of Olives.[38] Directly below
him were the cobbled paths winding between the reddish-grey rock
buildings, rambling down toward the pool of Siloam at the south end
of the city wall. His people were noisy as they hustled about selling,
gardening, cleaning, butchering, picking, trading, and cooking. He
loved his kingdom. Memories flooded his mind from the vantage
point where he stood. It was near the Gihon Spring water shaft just
below him, which had been his ticket into Jerusalem years before.
His own mighty men had climbed through this hewn-from-the-rock
secret passageway, entering the city from within and opening it to
David's army on the outside.

KING DAVID'S CITY

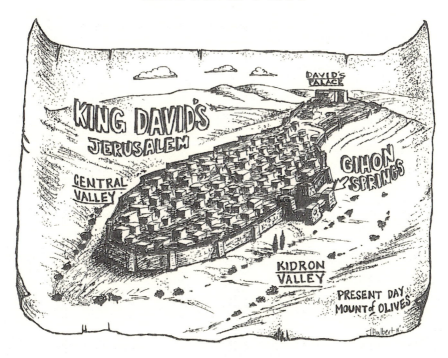

Yes, he had some great views from his palace. He could see all
that was his and even some things that weren't his to see. In a house

just below the terrace, he had an unobstructed view of the private life of a young married couple. A stunning young woman lived there, and he knew her husband was away at war. Was this why he stayed home?

David was watching her bathe. She may have been doing what all Jewish women did by performing what was called a mikvah,[39] a ritual cleansing. Perhaps she was in a room on the roof of the house. Either way, David could gaze at her every move. Perhaps this had become a secret habit of his, sneaking away at just the right time to enjoy this "innocent" pleasure unbeknownst to her.

He was infatuated with the form of this exquisite woman, and he had to have her. So, he decided he would make her an offer she couldn't refuse and sent for her. Maybe she, like other women in his past, would be attracted to his power and strength. After all, he was the king, and every woman knew you shouldn't say no to the king. This young lady was married to a foreigner, a Hittite who lived among the Jews.[40] He was loyal to his king and to Israel. We know this because he was listed as one the thirty-seven "crème of the crop" warriors, one of David's mighty men, Uriah the Hittite.[41]

I wonder if Uriah was among those who opened the city gate to David and Israel's forces so they could rush in and conquer the city?[42] Was this why his home was so close to David's terrace? Maybe he was "secret service," a special guard for the king. We know he was among the select thirty-seven of the mighty men. Wouldn't this be ironic? Uriah's job was to watch over the king, and now the king was watching over the person most precious to him—his wife Bathsheba.

If you read that list of select mighty men, you'll also see another interesting name there: Eliam of Giloh. Eliam fought with Uriah and was Bathsheba's father. Based on tradition and just plain

39. *Mikvah* means collection and refers to a collection of water used by the Jews for ceremonial washing. The Jews would purify themselves before certain activities or after events that made them unclean which for women included seven days after menstruation or childbirth. It is possible that this is what Bathsheba was doing. This is also the time that a woman is most fertile.
40. 1 Kings 9:20
41. 2 Samuel 23:39
42. 1 Chronicles 11:4-9 & 2 Samuel 5:6-8

old common sense, you don't marry your daughter off to someone you don't respect, especially someone you've worked and fought alongside of. Uriah was apparently a man of real integrity.

David not only had the love and support of his people; his mighty men wouldn't hesitate to die for him either. He had earned their respect, and now he was basking in the glow of that achievement. On this day though, as he stood alone with his heart pounding out of his chest in lustful anticipation, he cut off both God and friends to pursue his passion. God had blessed David. Together they had accomplished great things, yet he was shutting off the power that had enabled him to be a person of refuge by choosing his own pleasure over the well being of others. He wanted the warmth of this woman. Perhaps he had viewed her many times before, but this time he had to have her! This time he did more than look; he took the young bride of his trustworthy friend and personal guard.[43]

43. The speculation of the location of Bathsheba's roof is based on personal visits to the archaeological digs going on in David's city in the southeast part of Jerusalem. Further research on this subject and the developing story would be worth the effort on the part of the reader. This is an evolving discovery.

9

THE DANGER OF UNGUARDED ANONYMITY

David sinned; he squelched the influence of God and took advantage of his sister and brother. He allowed his unbridled desire to steal the object of Uriah's affection. He just wanted the comfort of this woman. Do we deserve to be happy? Not if, in attaining our happiness, we go against all that we know to be true. We can't comfort ourselves by deliberately denying what is right. We need to be Comforter-Reliant! We need to call out to God in times of temptation like this and remind Him that we want to do the right thing. But we're going to need some big-time help!

David discovered the age-old truth that satisfaction is elusive. Ask anyone in pursuit of it. When we try to find satisfaction in a physical connection with someone else, we'll end up disappointed. We are hardwired for much more than physical satisfaction. Our God-given need for intimacy can't be fulfilled only biologically; knowing someone spiritually, emotionally, and physically is the only way to operate in life the way God intended. If we keep giving into lust, the result will simply be a lust for more.[44] Isn't it interesting that even the advertising world understands this? A deep longing for more within every one of us is a pretty good indication that we were created for something more than what this world alone can offer. Maybe God has bigger plans for us all someday.

Someone once said, "It's not whether or not we sin that matters, but how we recover." Doesn't that ring true? Welcome to the human race. With the exception of Jesus, the Bible says all have sinned. The tendency is to parse and define sin by calling them mistakes or misjudgments or to grade sins, so, in comparison, I can feel better about myself by determining that your's is worse. It's best if

44. Romans 1:27

we simply own our stuff. When we do, we're on our way to becoming a person of refuge. Sin separates us from God, and this isn't a good idea. So how do we stay connected to God?

The Hebrew word for sin, *lo shema' lequol*, means to turn in on oneself. Before I show you what this looks like, we have to first get a picture of how we relate to God. Imagine a circle made up of three smaller circles with each one of them connected by an arrow coming out of each and going into the next one. In the top circle write the word "God." The arrow then comes out of the God circle and into the next one in which you'll write your name. Then out of that one (your name) comes another arrow penetrating the next circle, in which you'll write "others." Out of that circle draw an arrow coming out and going into the God circle. Got it? Here's a sketch of it.

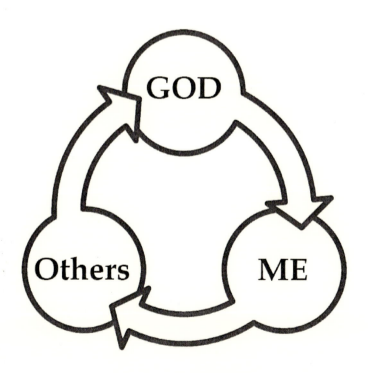

This is what life looks like. God created all of us in His image so we are naturally connected to him. We are also told in the first epistle of John that if we say we love God, we cannot hate our brother. Our arrows connect. Then we connect back to God. It's a continual movement, a holy dance about how life is supposed to work. Now, remember the Hebrew definition of sin? Take those arrows where your name is and make them both point back to you, away from God and others. That's sin. When it's all about me, it's sin. Period. Sin

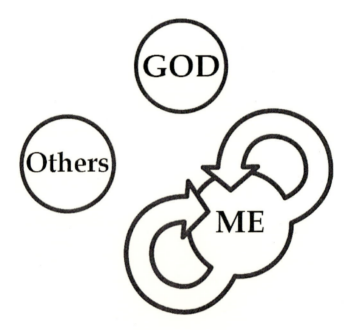

separates us from God and others.

The heart wrenching consequences of David's choice was that once the arrows pointed in on him, and Bathsheba discovered that

she was pregnant as a result of laying with David, it took a lot of repair work to get those arrows back to where they belonged. He tried
to hide it, but as a friend of mine, David Roper, likes to say, "God
loves us way too much to leave us alone." I guess that's what the Bible
means when it says our sin will find us out.[45]

Not to worry, David came up with a brilliant plan to cover his
sin. He sent for Uriah to come home from the battle to enjoy some
rest and a conjugal visit with his wife. But Uriah was loyal. This guy
wouldn't allow himself to enjoy something that his brothers in arms
still out on the battlefield couldn't, so he slept in front of David's
door on the floor instead! David was in an awful predicament. He
had to either come clean about this clandestine affair or have Uriah
killed to preserve his reputation. So David, the man after God's own
heart, chose murder instead of repentance. Did David really wrestle
with this choice, or had he buried the shame of his sin so deeply that
he no longer had the desire to look within? I don't know, but this
scares the heck out of me when I think about how easy it is to justify
my sinful actions.

Uriah returned to the front lines carrying the very order that
commanded his own ambush. So, as ordered by David, in the heat of
battle, the commander gave the order to retreat, leaving Uriah alone
on the battlefront. He was ambushed to cover up someone else's sin.
David made a *decision* to stop partnering with God. What he and
God had enjoyed together was now severed, but God wasn't giving
up on David. He sent Nathan the prophet to confront David, and he
did it with courage.

With no fear for his own life, Nathan confronted the king.
This could have been his final act! It takes guts to confront the king
who can demand your life with a snap of his fingers, but Nathan had
a strong distaste for injustice. He pointed his finger right at David.
Instead of denial, David melted in shame, owned his sin, and cried

out to God for mercy. The Bible says we are to "confess our sins and pray for each other that we might be healed."[46] Humble, honest confession is the way to healing. This is a major part of God's transformation process in our lives. After the prophet Nathan confronted David, his confession spilled out graphically and honestly.

Psalm fifty-one records his confession, and it's worth the read. It gave God room to cleanse, repair, and restore David's life. As many will vouch, the process of coming clean about our pain and sin is worth the embarrassment. For us to be a person of refuge we have to face the darkness within. If we do, then others who fear facing their deepest pain will find us safe. When they feel safe with us, they'll accept the God we believe in to be safe as well.

Unguarded anonymity resulted in horrifying consequences. It seems that swingin' the sword and staying in the battle is much better for us than being allowed to live alone and unaccountable. David left the influence of God, but God didn't leave David. He stayed with him until he finally bowed. Though we give up, God never does! Isn't that good news?

I wish partnership were similar to a lifetime membership; once you're in, you can just relax. But partnership has its privileges as well as its risks. We have a choice. We get to choose to partner with God, but that same choice allows us to breach the partnership like David did. Even when we go and do something stupid, we can recover. We don't have to spend the rest of our lives with "woulda-coulda-shoulda" thinking, regretting our wrong choices, even though we may think we're too far gone to be used by God again. Ask David how it worked out for him.

We can recover. God wants us back in the game. No, it won't be easy, and it may feel like a wrestling match with God. Like the Bible story about Jacob wrestling with an angel yet refusing to let go until he was blessed, we need that same tenacity. We have to believe—no—be totally persuaded that God's relentless affection for us allows us back in the game. If you're not persuaded, you'll need to pause and get this straightened out. Remember God's crazy about you. If I keep talking myself out of re-partnering with God, that's a me-problem not a God-problem. Self-punishment may at first appear to be humble, but it can actually be pride in disguise. Our disagreement with God's forgiveness of us is the same as telling God He doesn't know what He's doing. That's pride. We don't deserve to be called into partnership with God, but we *get* to because He has a relentless affection for us!

Let's get back to Jacob wrestling with that angel. He got his blessing, but not before he was smacked on the hip so hard he walked with a limp for the rest of his life. What a great reminder of his God-encounter. Every time he stood up, he'd wince and catch his breath remembering who was in charge. I have that same kind of limp. Every time I start walking off on my own, there's that dag-nab hitch in my gitty-up reminding me of whose I am. I have a serious limp. It's emotional. Well honestly, I have another one that a horse gave me once, but that's for another therapy session. My limp is a weakness that embarrasses me, but it's a constant reminder that I can't, nor was I designed to, do this thing on my own. I was designed for partnership with God. So were you.

10

EMBRACING A DANGEROUS OPPORTUNITY: MOVING FROM PAIN TO PURPOSE

My story didn't end with a diagnosis. I grappled with my depression and waded into the darkness with the help of a counselor. After two years of "exploring my pain," I left the ministry. I moved to Idaho and started building houses. Though I didn't know which end of the hammer to hold, my cousin Doug hired me onto his crew. I hammered and cut and joyfully labored until I cleared my head and heart. For three years, being able work with my hands enabled me to see a tangible result from my labor. I still love the smell of sawdust in the morning!

I began to unravel all that had bound me for so long and caught a glimpse of a God who was actually safe. This demanding perfectionist God that I had been trying so hard to appease was actually *not* the God of the Bible. I had been serving the wrong god! Maybe some atheists are right; they don't believe in God because the god they're familiar with doesn't really exist!

Through this time away from ministry, I discovered that I served people out of a deep need to be needed and validated. God and the Church had been synonymous for me, but now I realized they were not. One of them is perfect, and the other is a bride that is clearly not ready for her wedding day! I also discovered I wasn't as tough as I thought. I hated that. I couldn't handle the emotional pressure of ministry without help. Most importantly, I learned that God called me Jim, not Pastor Jim. He really did care, and He had heard my cry. He allowed me the opportunity to experience pain, and that pain brought about a resolve to undergo the transformation necessary for becoming a person of refuge.

I vividly recall those years in the wrestling match with God not knowing who was going to win. I feared that if I faced my questions head on, I would discover God was a sham and that true intellectual pursuit would end up in agnosticism or even atheism. As I struggled with God, there were times I was certain I had Him in a hold. But He would always twist away and out of reach from of my grip. Other times it seemed more like I was getting body-slammed. Sometimes, He'd squeeze me so tightly I could hardly breathe. I would slip away quickly, but He always outplayed me.

Then one day, in the midst of His horrific grip, I finally understood. His hold was just that, a hold. He wouldn't let go of me because He didn't *want* to let go of me! He was holding me through this storm, intending to never let go. I weep as I write these words because I still feel that squeeze. His love for me had nothing to do with my performance. He didn't love me because I was a good boy. He didn't allow pain in my life because He was cruel and unfair. Pain was becoming my teacher. God allowed it for the purpose of training me in perseverance so that I could hang in there until my soul was healed.

When I left full time ministry, I really didn't think I would ever come back. During the restoration period, I wondered what my calling in life really was. I've learned since that everyone's calling is simply to take the next right step. So after several of those steps, and knowing I still had a long way to go, I took another step. I was per-suaded that God was crazy about me, so with a few other "crazies" like me, we planted a church in a friend's living room.

We began with a small army of twelve, and half of them were under the age of ten. We were committed to meeting together and inviting folks who needed a refuge. A culture of wounded-but-healed people who believed that God was our refuge began to organize into a structure of refuge. It wasn't easy, but it really was that simple. We just kept gathering until eventually other people started coming. Nearly twenty years later, we still meet, and people still need a refuge. We were committed to being *people* of refuge. We've attempted to be a *church* of refuge too. Sometimes we've succeeded, and sometimes we've failed, but our focus has remained. I don't dislike the Church because I remember that Jesus calls us His bride and that it's supposed to be a holy militia.

As I watched this group we had gathered grow in number, I realized that this kind of soul healing was what God wanted for everyone. The ones who experience refuge are the best ones to share that hope of healing with others. Didn't Jesus say that? He who has been forgiven much loves much? Who better to share the hope of a healed life than someone who is being made whole? This is partnership with Him, to accept others as God does.

HOW ARE YOU DEALING WITH CRISIS?

Not everyone is a warrior by nature. Some simply don't identify with the fighting terminology in David's story. But struggle is common to us all isn't it? Some people calmly, and even skeptically, take their difficult questions to God and stay there until they get an answer, or at least some peace. Others tend toward cynicism and just stay in that rut of doubt.

Skepticism can be helpful in that it helps us examine things for what they truly are. Cynicism goes beyond that to a careless "stick it to the man" attitude that no longer cares about the facts. Cynicism can be one of the steps in struggling toward faith, but it is not the end game. Skeptics can be very wise, but cynics can simply be critics with no intention of resolution. The cynic can ask the questions, but he or she also needs to stick around until they get an answer. The "sticking around" is the fight I'm talking about. Not letting go until the Lord blesses is what this thing is all about. However you do it, stay by the stuff until you have peace.

The blessing that Jacob was after is what we need too. The Hebrew word for bless is *barak*. It has a double meaning. It can mean "to kneel," like kneeling before a king. It can also mean "bring a gift to another *while* kneeling." The blessing of God is indeed a gift, and we need that touch from Him. If blessing means kneeling and God is the one blessing, does that mean He kneels in front of us? Though I'm uncomfortable with the idea of God kneeling in front of us, I realize He, in fact, did come down to our level to demonstrate His affection toward us.[47] When He blesses, *He* kneels because He loves us that much. I guess He really is crazy about us.

Do you want what God offers? Do you want His blessing, and are you willing to wrestle until you have it? Are you willing to limp? Are you willing to have scars? Are you willing to go into eternity a little more fragile if it means you really connect with the living God? I'm at a point where I don't trust a leader who *doesn't* limp.

Maybe this is why the Apostle Paul boasted in his weakness. When he did, he was bragging on God's strength that was being perfected and matured in him.[48] No matter who I am or what I've done, if I come clean before God and open myself to His transforming presence, He steps into my weakness and qualifies me for the task!

47. Philippians 2:5-11
48. 2 Corinthians 12:9

11

EVERYTHING I NEEDED TO KNOW
I LEARNED IN A CAVE

Okay, you've heard my story. If you talk to people who know me, you'll get mixed reviews. Some will tell you that I'm not perfect, that I really believe this stuff, and that I am serious about being a person of refuge. Others will tell you that I'm too direct, or that I've offended them. That's because sometimes I *am* too direct and I *am* offensive! I am genuinely sorry for that and believe I've seen personal progress as Jesus continues to "wrench" on me as my personal mechanic. He's helping me to be loving enough to be truthful and direct yet sensitive and considerate as well.

I could make a list right now of all the places I fall short, but I'll save you the boredom. How about you? Are you acutely aware of your weaknesses and failures? Welcome to the club. You're not yet what you will be, and you're journeying alongside good company. Being a person of refuge is about being *transformed*. The Bible says we are being transformed daily.[49] If your imperfection is going to keep you from partnering with God, then you'll never partner. Who are we? What are we going to live for? For stuff? For fame? For people's approval? I learned long ago that I can't make everyone happy; you can't either, but we *can* make God smile! Getting the "following Jesus thing" down pat will take me all the way to my graduation day. So I'm going to relax, trust Him, and enjoy the journey. God enjoys it when we lean on Him for help.

Are you shooting straight with yourself and others? Are you choosing unguarded anonymity, or are you staying in the game and swingin' the sword? Those who limp will all agree that the struggle is

49. 2 Corinthians 3:18

worth it. God is found in the midst of the pain, but it might be a long night. Hang in there and don't give up. *Don't waste your pain by not learning from it.*

Don't worry that being a person of refuge means you need to sign up for a degree in pain. Maybe you've already done the homework! Maybe it's just a matter of letting Jesus take you back through what you've already experienced to show you how He can use it to mature you. Please friend, don't shrink away from the struggle; you might be closer to hope than you think.

Please allow me to share some thoughts about how to become a person of refuge.

1. *It's not about me*: If you're a leader who's been dragged off or has fallen off the pedestal of leadership, thank God. Pedestals are stupid places to try and lead from. Sometimes people put us there, and sometimes we climb up ourselves. Pedestals can be tempting because of the power they offer, but we're not about pointing to ourselves. We want to point everyone to Jesus. Besides, who needs that kind of pressure anyway?

2. *Everyone has influence*: In other words, we all lead. Whether one person follows us or thousands, we have influence in someone's life. Honest, broken, and healed people can have great influence for good, so don't fall into the trap of thinking you can't be an influence or refuge for people. God has humbled Himself to love you and me, and He did it for a reason, so don't waste it.

3. *Own it, confess, and get back on track*: Some of us have sinned under the radar and not been caught. Some of us have been exposed to public humility, trapped in our transgressions. Either way, all of us have sinned. Let's call it what it is and not cover it up with excuses. There's an epidemic of narcissism in our culture. It is filled with those who don't own their sin,

blame, and dodge. A deep conviction of sin and remorse is known as Godly sorrow.[50] That's a great thing. Let it lead you to the feet of Jesus. You'll never make a heavenly impact until you do.

4. *Let your pain inform you*: If you've been sinned against, I truly am sorry. This can derail a sense of purpose as much as anything. Our embarrassment can cause us to hide, quit, or run. We can easily feel like our usefulness is over, and that no one, including God, has noticed our absence. Anger can well up, both toward God who allowed the pain and towards those who smugly used us to their own end. Becoming a person of refuge may seem too dangerous or costly. It is dangerous! But facing the pain will open your heart to the real God of refuge who longs to hold you. Please enter the struggle and stay until you have the blessing of peace.

5. *Life is tough*: "Life is good" makes a great bumper sticker, but frankly, sometimes life stinks. I'm not immune to the struggles common to all people, and neither are you. Theologies that tell us living the victorious life means freedom from the struggle don't work. Try telling this theology to Jesus. Maybe you've heard about Isaiah, the prophet whose own son-in-law sawed him in half from the groin up. Or what about Job, who lost his family and fortune, and John the Baptist, who got the people ready for Jesus' arrival only to be killed just as Jesus began to minister? Then there was Stephen who was stoned to death followed by other martyrs Paul, Peter, and James. What about the current day believers in Africa, Asia, and the Middle East? Pain allows us to lead from humility. Humility allows people to look past us to see Jesus, the real refuge. Life is good only when you're a partner with God.

6. *A person of refuge still speaks the truth*: Jesus came in truth

and love. Usually we're better at one than the other, but we need both. We need refuge, but we also need to be transformed. Love is the refuge, and transformation can only happen when we face the truth.

I need to exercise humility and allow those I trust, who are also being transformed, to speak truth into my life. *Be cautious of the ones who want to speak truth into your life while refusing to be transformed themselves.* You can't have one without the other.

I apologize in advance for the offense I'm about to cause, but there was another cave in the Bible too. This one was also a hiding spot for David and his men while Saul was pursuing him.[51] Saul came into the cave of EnGedi and relieved himself. It's an interesting story with a powerful parallel. Some people look for a cave for reasons other than wanting hope. They will use the refuge you provide for their own purposes, not caring about who gets dumped on, which leads me to the next point. We need to provide caves of refuge, not refuse!

7. *Being a person of refuge is risky for the heart*: Saul betrayed David. The wound for David was deep, and it caused a legitimate fear. David was fearful of opening up and trusting others. I get this, don't you? In First Chronicles chapter twelve, verse sixteen, an important exchange happens between David and one of the men gathered with him in the cave of Adullam. David, leery of being hurt again, said, "If you have come to me in friendship to help me, my heart will be joined to yours, but if you betray me to my adversaries, although there is no wrong in my hands, then may the God of our fathers see and rebuke you."

There's no greater pain than to be betrayed by someone you've opened your life to and provided refuge for. A man named Amasai replied to David's concern with these words: "We are yours, O David, and with you, O son of Jesse. Peace, peace to you and peace to your helpers for your God helps you." David received Amasai and the men with him and made them officers in his army. There will be people who hurt you. Like David though, we can heal from that hurt and risk again. We need to receive refuge as much as we need to give refuge. I have people like this in my life. I hope you do too. Take the risk!

8. *Lead with a limp*: If you've wrestled with God or are in the midst of the fight, stay with it. Trust that you will come to a place of understanding and contentment. At this point, you will also absolutely know you cannot make it on your own. Your weaknesses may be glaring, and your failures may be embarrassing, but this is the stuff of humility. Humility and humiliation come from the same root word, so don't be surprised if others see the real you.

   This limp is the real you; it's the thing you can't hide and the daily reminder that you are designed to partner with God. Unguarded anonymity doesn't work—it's too dangerous. If God can use my painful story, he can use yours too. We have nothing left to lose, right? Let's be open because our candor and authenticity will be like a refuge of understanding and safety for others.

9. *Grace is needed every day*: People of refuge know that grace is the fuel they need for daily living. Grace is not only for the moment of initial forgiveness. We live *because* of grace, and we live *by* grace. Grace means "gift" or unearned favor. God wants to give us His unearned favor and power even though we can't earn it. It's there for the asking, enjoy it. Being a person of refuge isn't easy, and it will require more strength,

wisdom, and grace than you're capable of coming up with yourself, but you'll find that all the grace you need will be there in abundance!

10. *Don't forget that this is a "get to" not a "have to"*: Living this way is a privilege not drudgery. If you don't want to be empowered and used to impact others for good, you don't have to. I'll never forget climbing up the side of Mt. Arbel in the Galilee of Israel and seeing the view from the top. The ancient road below us was called the Via Maris. It was an ancient trade route that led south into Africa. It intersected nearby with the routes that led to both Asia and Europe. It was the crossroads of the world! Jesus led his disciples to this place where as many as four thousand people a day passed by. From this vantage point, He gave them what has been called the Great Commission! He told them to go into the whole world and teach the things He had taught them. The word Jesus used for world was ethne. We interpret it as ethnicity. Jesus was watching humanity from every corner of the world pass by when he said this. We get to merge with the world while possessing the great news of God's deep affection and His call to love each other. Oh and by the way, the meaning of Arbel is "God's ambush." He's ambushing the world with transformed people of refuge!

SO LET'S GET REAL, OK?

To be candid, looking back on my own story, the thought of asking a counselor to help me was humiliating. I finally reasoned, "Okay, I'll go a few times for some pointers, and then I'll do it on my own." Two years later I was dreading the day when I would have to say goodbye to this person who had shown me true refuge. One afternoon, as I sat in my little vintage Buick convertible (I was depressed, not lacking in taste of fine vintage cars) and talked to God. I said, "Of course this is painful, Lord, but I've learned so much, I'll take whatever you want to throw at me. Just don't stop teaching me!"

My view of struggling had clearly changed. I didn't care anymore that I was weak. I actually no longer cared if it hurt. I just wanted to hang on because I was learning so much about God and myself. I was holding on until I was blessed!

Maybe the thought of facing the pain is like walking into the "dark night of the soul," as Saint John of the Cross called it. Maybe you believe that if you reveal the real you, God and those who love you will be disappointed. God will be thrilled about your honesty. In fact, it's here that He does His best work. Coming to the end of ourselves can feel devastating, but it opens us up to the healing that God wants for us.

12

WHAT HAPPENS IN ADULLAM, LEAVES ADULLAM!

What happens when two or three people of refuge get together? The place they gather becomes a place of refuge. If God is my refuge, and I am being transformed, then I will leave the cave and partner with God. I partner with God when I open my life to others, so they can find refuge. That's it. When we partner, our families, our workplaces, and our churches will be places of refuge.

Over the years of wrestling with the theology of refuge, I've come to understand that a *place* of refuge is built by *people* of refuge one relationship at a time. This isn't a formula; it's a culture. If the culture emerges, then a structure can be built to uphold the vision of being a place of refuge. When people of refuge gather in community, it can have an amazing impact. Here's the bottom line: *we cannot have places of refuge, if we aren't first people of refuge.* Refuge theology is a call to authenticity and Spirit-enabled maturity. When I answer that call, I move from pain to purpose. It must start with me. If it moves to you, we will have the beginnings of an ecclesia—a holy militia!

There is a story about a pastor in the 1960's who became a person of refuge to a generation of outcasts. It's also a story about motorcycles, and I like motorcycles, but I digress. This is a powerful example of how a loving heart and a little ingenuity can make a big impact on the life of someone else.

THE VICAR IN A BLACK LEATHER JACKET

Reverend Bill Shergold, an Anglican pastor in London,

England, loved the people in his parish, but he noticed a group of young people that society and the church had turned away. He decided to do something about it. In 1959, the city of London was not friendly to the many leather-clad, motorcycle-riding teenagers that tore through its narrow cobble-stoned streets. These "hooligans" were not welcome in roadside restaurants, cinemas, or even bowling alleys. The only place they could gather was at the Ace Café in London.

One day, the good reverend decided to climb onto his Triumph motorcycle and ride down to the café to see if he could connect with these young people. The first time he timidly approached the café, he sped up and drove past out of fear for his own life. He finally worked up the courage and went back. This time he climbed off of his bike and began to mingle among the café-racers. He was shocked to find that the kids liked him and even respected him for hanging out. Sometime after that initial meeting, he invited this pack of rowdy teenagers to his church. He had planned a special biker service just for them.

The young people took to Father Bill, affectionately referring to him as the "biker priest." They rode in droves to the Saturday night meeting. Before long they gathered regularly at the church calling themselves "the 59 Club." Father Bill even had a special rally for the club members calling it "the blessing of the bikes." At this rally, Father Bill compared these young people to the "knights of old," urging them to use their bikes for God's service by becoming young men and women of integrity.

The 59 Club still exists today with over forty-thousand members worldwide! In fact, I'm a member. When some of the original club members were asked about Father Bill, they verified countless stories of how their lives had drastically changed direction because of Father Bill's influence. The vicar in a black leather jacket loved the kids that no one else accepted. The result is that he changed their lives for good. Father Bill was a person of refuge. He is held in high regard as a man who changed the lives of a forgotten generation. He is a legend among motorcycle enthusiasts worldwide and a great example of someone who lived in partnership with God in order to touch lives. I wonder: what will our generation say about us?

I'm finally beginning to understand that I can't make it on my own. I need God and others like Father Bill who will encourage me and remind me to live the way I was designed to live! Depression never goes too far away. It seems to hover on the horizon occasionally poking its ugly head above the skyline to glare at me with its fiery eyes. I'm constantly aware of how weak I am all by myself. God provides me with what I need to keep this enemy at bay, but it requires an utter dependence on Him for the power to do so.

I am the product of all the people in my life, healthy and unhealthy, who have either encouraged my transformation or forced me to the throne room of God to find grace to help in time of need. Don't worry; this isn't an invitation to suffer. I actually hate pain, but I have prayed that God would grant me grace to handle whatever comes my way. I've watched Him do this for so many others whose maturity and beauty shines in the midst of the struggle. I want to be that kind of person.

So, do you need a cave right now? Do you long for the God of refuge, but the pain has kept you from his embrace? If so, please make the journey. *Rest in His presence and get to know Him deeply from the heart.* There's no rush. Just start the journey and stay committed through the struggle. It will all be worth it.

Or, maybe it's time for you to leave the cave. It's interesting to note that not once did David's mighty men suggest they make the cave a little cozier; no one suggested wallpaper or curtains. They only stayed long enough to begin the transformation process. We aren't supposed to be cave-dwellers, we are supposed to walk with the King and fight the battles He gives us. Our identity can't be our story from the past. Our identity is how we partner with God.

David started well, but to start well doesn't guarantee a good finish. The journey will be fraught with triumphs and defeats. Some battles will be won while others will be lost. Good days will stand alongside the bad ones. We must commit to not fighting alone and remember to not let failure disable us. It will keep us humble so that when God uses us, we won't start believing our own press! First Kings records an interesting verse reflecting on the whole life of David. It says, "For David had done what was right in the eyes of the LORD and had not failed to keep any of the LORD's commands all the days of his life—*except* in the case of Uriah the Hittite."[52]

Except. That word "except" has kept so many from darkening the doors of God's presence. I've heard people say, "I'd turn to God except…" Or, "I know He loves me, and He could have used me except…" If we feel "convicted" by our past, remember the Spirit doesn't convict us to reject us. He convicts out of love, longing to restore us and to bring us into His service. Please don't be one of the people who lets the word "except" keep you from becoming an authentic person of refuge. Though we're not perfect, let's stay in the game for the whole game, and let's celebrate together at the victory party!

I heard there's a cave just over the hill, and it's a safe place to heal and move from pain to purpose. Let's go there together, okay?

ACKNOWLEDGEMENTS

I want to say thanks to a few people of refuge. My wife, Dori, is my partner, co-pastor, and often the voice of reason for me. No one has encouraged me to press on like she has. She has definitely been a person of refuge to me as she stuck by me as I stumbled into the cave of God's refuge. I dedicate this book to her.

Psalm 127:3 tells us "children are a gift from the Lord…" Zac, Charissa, and Makenzie have inspired me, humbled me, and made me proud. Specifically I thank Zac for the wonderful cover design, Sheena Israel, his wife, who has continued to inspire my study of our Jewish roots, and Makenzie for the editing and encouragement of my writing. I also want to thank Matthew Howen who designed the interior of the book, Beth Stockett for her keen editing skills, and Jeannie Keneley, my assistant and sister, who whittled down my original manuscript and managed this publishing project. This was a team effort, and I couldn't have done without you all, thanks!

Dr. Sarah Sumner, you've been a great friend and honest authenticator. Your challenges, encouragement, and affirmation have been insightful. Thanks so much.

To Bill and Jody Buckner, who honored me by writing the foreword for this book. I want to express my deepest appreciation. You've known the pain of deep suffering, and you live as a refuge for others. You model for us what it means to be people of refuge.

Thank you to my Mom and Dad for your support and, above all else, teaching us kids radical faith. To my sisters who passed up countless opportunities to smother me (and I don't mean with love), thank you for all your support and love and for reminding me that "I can do all things through Him who gives me strength." Dori's family received me like one of their own, supporting and encouraging me even while moving their daughter, sister, and grandkids all over creation on our assignments and wanderings. I am grateful for you all!

To the original gang of twelve who started Crossroads with us in the Dille's living room back in January of 1996, you know who you are, and we love you. You helped me understand what people of refuge looked like. Thank you.

To the amazing, gifted staff of Crossroads, I can't say enough about your impact on my family's life. I can't name you all, but you have been true and faithful friends and family. You've created space for me to pursue this project. You have smoothed my rough edges and even polished those places I thought were already finely carved. You've protected me, but insisted I keep swinging the sword. You've been people of refuge to Dori and me, and our lives are rich because of you.

Thanks to Judi, George, John, Jerry and Jackie, my personal prayer team over the past umpteen years. God has used you greatly! Thanks!

I have to thank David Roper. As a friend, pastor and mentor, you're the one who first steered me in the direction of understanding the metaphor of David and his mighty men as an example of real refuge. You have been a person of refuge for many of us pastors here in Idaho. Thanks.

Last but not least, the family of Crossroads Community Church has been the greatest source of encouragement to us in our journey with Christ. You've journeyed with us, stood beside us, and most importantly laughed at most of my jokes. This pastorate isn't my career, it's my passion, and you have helped make me what I am. I will always be appreciative to each of you and the part you've played in making the world a little friendlier, more graceful, and manageable. Thank you for demonstrating what it means to be people of refuge!

I hope that I will be a person of refuge like Jesus has been to me.

Jim Halbert

Now unto him who is able to do immeasurably more than all we ask or imagine, according to his power that is at work within us, to him be glory in the church and in Christ Jesus throughout all generations, for ever and ever! (And all of God's people said...) Amen.

Ephesians 3:20

FACEBOOK & MORE

Follow Jim on his facebook page:
http://www.facebook.com/RefugeJimHalbert
Or just search for Refuge, Jim Halbert

Also, visit
www.JimHalbert.org

Thanks